VOICES

CULTURE AND PERFORMANCE SERIES

General Editor

Frank E. Manning

Associate Editor

Ray B. Browne

VOICES

An Anthropologist's Dialogue
with an Italian-American Festival

RICHARD M. SWIDERSKI

Bowling Green State University Popular Press
Bowling Green, OH 43403

Centre for Social and Humanistic Studies
University of Western Ontario
London, Ontario

Copyright © 1987 by Bowling Green State University Popular Press

Published in the United States by the
Bowling Green State University Popular Press
Bowling Green, Ohio 43403

Published in Canada by the
Centre for Social and Humanistic Studies
University of Western Ontario
London, Ontario N6A 5C2

Library of Congress Catalogue Card No.: 86-72486

ISBN: 0-87972-364-5 Clothbound
0-87972-365-3 Paperback

To Pat

Cia beimmi a-min nach ré
nï derban cách a chèle:
    maith la cechtar nár a dán;
    subaighthius a óenurán.

Foreword

Cultural performances have in recent years attracted renewed attention from various quarters of the social sciences and the humanities Their study, moreover, has crossed, redrawn, and all but obliterated many conventional academic boundaries. The *Culture and Performance* series is a response to this challenging development. The series offers a topical forum for the publication of wide-ranging scholarship on the ethnography and theory of ritual, drama, festivity, sport, entertainment, ceremony, spectacle, and other popular forms of collective symbolic expression. Approaches vary but share the central aim of contributing to the social and humanistic study of performance.

The St. Peter's Fiesta, a four-day celebration held annually by Italian Americans in Gloucester, Massachusetts, is a rich medley of symbolic types. It is—to limn its highlights only—a religious devotion, and ethnic and fishing festival, a family and community feast, an amusement-based carnival, a sports tournament, a political ceremony, and a tourist attraction. Each of these 'voices' speaks to anthropologist Richard Swiderski, who strives to hear them both as separate sounds and as tones within a chorus that strikes dissonance as often as it achieves harmony. Like MacAloon (1981) in his recent work on the Olympic Games, Swiderski brillantly shows how a single cultural performance can encompass a variety of symbolic forms, each replete with its own meanings and metameanings.

If the St. Peter's Fiesta speaks in multiple voices, Swiderski's account of it exemplifies what Geertz (1980) artfully calls the "blurring" of genres. Here the blur is between anthropology and history. Conventionally, anthropologists have taken the license of writing in the ethnographic present. Events observed at a point in time are described as timeless and analysed as part of a synchronic system rather than in relation to changing temporal circumstances.

vii

Historians, of course, have done much the opposite, resulting in a wide separation between disciplines that, otherwise, have much in common.

Interestingly, the investigation of performances in popular culture is an area where anthropology and history have recently converged in ways that portend a promising dialogue. Representative studies in anthropology include, on a macro level, Turner and Turner's (1978) work on Latin American and European pilgrimage traditions and, on a micro level, Cohen's (1980) analysis of the London Carnival between 1965 and 1980. In history, there is Ladurie's (1979) splendid study of the 1580 Mardi Gras Carnival in Romans, France, and Davis' (1984) interpretation of specific charivaris in Geneva and Lyon in the seventeenth century. Such efforts throw light on processes and events, remote and recent.

Swiderski's study focuses on the 1970 performance of the St. Peter's Fiesta. It was a year of crisis for the festival, which was almost cancelled, and for the community, which was in a state of disillusionment and indifference. A Catholic school had been closed, the fishery was being devastated, a traditional sense of bounded ethnicity was rapidly dissolving, and a mounting toll of sons and brothers were being claimed by the war in Vietnam. With its cultural lifelines cut, festivity is drained of the aesthetic appeal and contagious spirit that we ideally attribute to it. Instead, it is strained, disoriented, jarring in its rendition and unsettling, even traumatic, in its aftermath.

Swiderski approaches the St. Peter's Fiesta in relation to both its social context and its performance history. Drawing inspiration from Bakhtin and Rabelais, Swiderski is sensitive to the grotesque polyphony of his surroundings and to the absurd incongruity of his own role as an anthropologist. His response is poetically appropriate—a work that is consciously ironic, parodically reflective, and often playfully at odds with its own "academic" objectives. The St. Peter's Fiesta is here enriched by another voice, resonant throughout the following pages and likely reverberative in future studies of cultural performance.

FRANK E. MANNING

University of Western Ontario

Contents

Preface

This is a study of the St. Peter's Fiesta celebrated annually by the Italian- or better, Sicilian-American community of Gloucester, Massachusetts, USA. The study deals specifically with the fiesta that took place on 25-28 June 1970, although I am broadly concerned with previous and subsequent performances.

Why study such an event?

The St. Peter's Fiesta is a good example of a festival that features several different kinds of festivity at the same time. It is an ethnic festival in a plural society; it is a fishermen's festival, a Roman Catholic saint's festival, and an Old World festival recreated in a new environment. It is also a tourist festival and a regional festival. Identity, livelihood, religion, and tradition coverage—and often conflict—in the celebration.

Calendrical festivals are intense events that occur at one moment of the year, but spread their influence over the entire year. When the St. Peter's Fiesta began in the 1920s, the fishing boats—the "Italian fleet"—were making their first expeditions into the deep waters of Georges Banks, marking a turning point in the region's (and the Italian community's) yearly economic cycle. That the boats cannot or do not make such expeditions any longer lends the festival added, not less, significance. When the festival was formed, Gloucester was a major fishing port. Its fishing people contributed greatly to the legendry, technology, and economics of the Atlantic fisheries. The St. Peter's Fiesta belongs to Gloucester and to the North Atlantic fisheries. It is celebrated at the common point of several spheres of Gloucester and North Atlantic life. How the festival carries all these meanings at the same time gives it interest. A close look at the St. Peter's Fiesta reveals how festivals are shaped and how wide are the constituencies of such seemingly special events.

But why the 1970 performance of the festival? The social importance of that year is discussed at length in the following pages. More generally, I believe that festivals must be studied as single events if they are to be understood at all. Unlike a literary work, a political movement, a social system, or a myth, a festival is its own moment, its own singularity. The more successfully the singularity is described, the more successfully the celebration is described. General attributes might evoke the celebration of, say, The Fourth of July in its fireworks, or Christmas in its gift exchanges, but as celebrations even these events happen locally and singularly. Their national or regional nature is a fiction maintained within the local celebration.

In part, then, the significance of 1970 is that the temporal distance between then and now helps to accentuate the specificity of the fiesta that took place in that year. Looking back, we see a fiesta that is not an eternal form but a product—and, of course, a revelation—of its disquieting time.

Historical distance also facilitates a second objective of this book—to balance ethnography with phenomenology. I am interested both in investigating a festival and in recounting the irreducible experience of "going to" and "being at" a festival. In this latter aim my method as fieldworker and writer is similar to that of the French anthropologist Colette Petonnet in her recent study of people passing through a cemetery (1982). She sat still and allowed the mood to take her along, terming the procedure *l'observation flottante*. I suspect that this passive, non-intrusive method, neither participation nor observation, has come into being (if not become popular) in the aftermath of aggressive colonial anthropology, whose confessory final gasp we have been hearing. Perhaps too, although I readily submit to correction on this point, this method has emerged with an increase in the feminist consciousness of anthropologists. If so, I hope that feminist theory is guide and mentor for its further development.

Acknowledgements

Individual authorship is an illusion, but one which the individual author relinquishes hesitantly. Many people have been involved in the development of this book. The present text is by no means the final result of this development nor the cumulative responsibility of these people; it is just the text which publication has caught. I can avoid the danger of autobiography by concentrating my thanks on those responsible for the present appearance.

The observations of the 1970 Festival at the core of the book were completed on a grant from the Center for Urban Ethnography at the University of Pennsylvania. But the grant was second to the assistance of my then wife, Mary Kay Mulligan, and, from inside the Gloucester Italian community, the advice of Irving Tebo, secretary of the St. Peter's Club. In the intervening years the book came near publication twice, but each time I did not like the conditions and balked. This is where the autobiography is eliminated. It was only when I submitted the manuscript to Frank Manning for the *Culture and Performance* series that I found an editor able to manage its reworking. Over the period of a year and more I submitted revised versions, received criticisms from Manning and the series' readers, and acted upon the criticisms and my own reactions to the readers' reactions. My anarchic intent has been rendered legible, and placed within the series. Frank Manning deserves credit for the face this text now shows, but not blame for what lies behind the facade. Rewriting also inspired me to return to Gloucester for the 1985 Fiesta, but the diversions of life again intervened and I have my good friend Pat Moran to thank for visiting the 1985 Fiesta scene and for bringing back information and photographs.

At the Centre for Social and Humanistic Studies, Rosemary Morris proved an efficient editorial assistant, careful copy reader, and conscientious correspondent. I am also grateful to Joyce G. Kissoon, who painstakingly did all the typesetting and helped in other ways too numerous to mention, and to Sonia Paine, who did a fine job of copyediting.

Publication of this volume has been assisted by generous grants from the Marconi Club of London (Ontario) and an enthusiast of the St. Peter's Fiesta who chooses to remain anonymous. I am deeply grateful to both benefactors.

Richard W. Swiderski

Bridgewater State University

PART ONE

UNDERTONES

CHAPTER 1

Reflections

In the work of Dostoyevsky, the world of the novel rises up to envelop the writer. His voice is one of a medley, even though it is the medium through which all of the others are heard. The similarity of the novel and carnival, a theme developed by Bakhtin (1973), suggests a comparison between Dostoyevsky and the ethnographer of festivity. Surrounded by a carnivalesque chorus, the ethnographer strives to listen and repeat, and then to add a voice of interpretation to the overwhelming polyphony. That interpretive voice, plural and variant in form, makes the first sound here, and then becomes a reflective background for the festive performance.

Festival as Text

The dogged reader finds 'texts' everywhere. All written works, societies, paintings, wars and lives are texts ready to be read and interpreted. Cultures are made of texts: "The culture of a people is an ensemble of texts, themselves ensembles, which the anthropologist strains to read over the shoulders of those to whom they properly belong" (Geertz 1972:452).

The history of ethnographers reading over shoulders, from the nose-thrusting Malinowski (1922) to the much more polite Dennis Tedlock (1983), is the history of a wish anthropologists long to have fulfilled: the culture already written out and, even if copyrighted by natives versed in the legalities, at least an open book before the critical eye. This conception of culture places anthropology squarely amid the humanities. The head-counting of survey research or the graphs of economics do not threaten the interpretive calm of reading along with the subject.

3

The festival is one text in the culture's ensemble. It can be read independently of the other texts or in conjunction with any number of them. Alternately, to use the word Geertz prefers, it can be "interpreted"

A festival text can be interpreted or read as a textual microcosm of the social and cultural macrocosm, or, to evoke a felicitous parallelism of English and other European languages, a text of the context. Its lines of action fasten together symbols referring systematically to the state of the culture. The reader stares at the festival over the shoulder of a participant and learns what it says. His / her reading is like the participant's participation. One phrase, or phase, follows another in sequences matching the unfolding life of the culture around. The signs and symbols do the work of alignment.

Reading festivals as one text or another is the standard form of festival analysis today. The textual reading is not just a voice but the entire act of understanding the festival, of which the primary object is the reduction to a text. Offering a definitive interpretation of the resultant text is an aspiration.

Native readers of festival texts always want to see the ideals of the culture expressed there: that is the theme of speeches during the festival itself and of wholesome articles afterward. Folklorists and anthropologists make something else of reading. William Lloyd Warner (1959) was reading American Memorial Day ceremonies as cultural texts before the idea of textuality was expressed. He read the ceremonial movement as affirmation of social and political boundaries to which festival-goers were unlikely to confess. The development of realistic reading soon undercut this idealistic reading: the festival was read to show the culture as it really was. Rappaport (1968) looked upon the pig feasts of Highland New Guinea peoples as texts of culture coping with environment. Abrahams (1972) ingeniously contrasted two separate festivals, Christmas and Carnival on the Caribbean island of St. Vincent, as a system of two kinds of texts, the one idealistic and the other realistic.

One further refinement in interpreting festival text was made once readers understood that the participants were themselves reading the festival and conditioning their participation by a specific reading. Lavenda (1983), referring to Geertz' cockfight article, contrasted a pair of Minnesota community festivals and found not only that they were metasocial texts of their respective towns but also that in one the text was "not a straightforward reflection of social structure" in the town.

> Rather, it seems to have been part of a series of adjustments, interpretations if you will, concerning the best way to achieve what virtually all agreed was the basic meaning of the festival. Once the adjustments were made, with the text not only reinterpreted but also revised, the new interpretations became potent. That the change had been made at all told people something of importance. For the power of a text is precisely that it is said—whether the frame be fiction, play, or jest (1983:64).

Lavenda, faithfully carrying out Geertz' program, gives the text a voice. The voice does not always announce the culture in so many words. Its *act* of speaking, of being a text, is the meaningful event.

Another strain in the interpretation of the festival text is, then, situating the text itself in a system of discourse. Here the reader allows the festival to be a text unto itself, divorced from strict realistic or idealistic correspondence to the culture. The festival-as-text expresses an aspect of the culture perhaps not otherwise expressed. The native over whose shoulder the anthropologist reads is reading too.

Akos Ostor (1980), examining the festivals of Durgapuja and Gajun in a Bengali town, found that these two festivals do not replicate common cultural meanings within their space and time, but are the templates of large-scale social relationships. Ostor's own theory is functionalist: the unique festival texts fill a role in the miscellany of town life. Seeing the text does not close the theory, but locates an artifact that helps complete the theory. All textualizing of festivals ends in function, acknowledged or unacknowledged, precisely because in being a text a festival is an item that must fit into the culture. Focusing upon the text, the reader expects the culture to be orderly around him/her. Geertz, Warner, Rappaport, Lavenda and Ostor are in agreement in expecting or at least allowing this to happen. Reading the festival text as an anthropological study seems to include the encompassing assumption that anthropology predicates function. Even when the text is just uttered it is uttered somewhere. When the text is a unique utterance, its reading relies on an expectation of functional fit.

Functionalism is the backlash of textuality. Instinctively, we seek the different orders of function whenever there is a cultural text before us. Walens' (1981) Kwakiutl live in a fully textual world bound by systems of analogy, homology, construction, and deconstruction. Their festivals, ceremonies, myths and lives are woven together in patterns more typical of literary works than of anthropologists' cultures. Walens has defeated the functional bias of reading texts by giving in to it entirely. The Kwakiutl he studies were texts from the start: his chief source of information is Franz Boas' and George Hunt's Kwakiutl writings. The original written nature of these texts supports a rhetorical analysis. Walens provides guidance to solve the problem of festival textuality. The festival and the entire culture around it may actually be texts and thus a field for critical argument long after the festivals themselves are gone.

Festival texts can correspond to a vague outside or be things in themselves, but as texts they face the consequences of textuality, which takes precedence over all else. As texts festivals can be constructed or deconstructed, since privileged interpreters or just anyone can read them and generate revised editions. The texts invariably lie within a niche, among other texts or objects, playing their functional part. Lying open on the festival ground, the text has a rich and full voice because it has many tones and keys. Allowing it to be a voice among others controls its functional ultimacy. It is just a text.

Festival as Play

The voice of play best starts with an anecdote. Some years ago, while waiting to be admitted to a tea ceremony, I fell into conversation with a man who had just visited Disneyland and was proclaiming its joys. I launched into a pedantic explanation of how and why the place is symbolic of American culture. The man would have none of this: "It's just a lot of fun," he said. Seeing a shortcut through my pedantry, I agreed and continued explaining that it is symbolic of American culture. "No, no," he interrupted, "it's **just** a lot of fun." "Oh," I said. A woman standing nearby smiled acutely. I suspect Jean Renoir was directing.

Play is opposed to interpretation; the played festival is not the read festival. The voice of play tries to outshout the voice of interpretation even as the interpreter makes this shouting the subject of his interpretation (cf. Lavenda 1983:51). Playing is simpler than interpreting: it is what the festival is and not what it is about. The call to festive play is a call away from serious reflection to unreflecting participation in mad rejoicing, L'Allegro replacing Il Penseroso.

Svetlana Alpers (1983), dissenting from the iconological bias of much recent art history, has proposed "two modes of representation that are central to Western art."

> As an example of the first, Albertian model we might keep in our mind's eye a work such as Titian's Venus of Urbino. The artist is a viewer who is actively looking out at objects-preferably human figures-in space, figures whose appearance, considered as a matter of size, is a function of their distance from the viewer. For the second, which I call the northern or descriptive mode, think of Vermeer's View of Delft. A fragment of the larger world is compressed into a piece of canvas, impressing its surface with color and light without taking the position of a viewer external to it into account. No scale or human measure is assumed (Alpers 1983:37).

The first mode of representation is Geertz' cultural text read over the shoulder; the second is the assertion of ordinary play. The match of an art historian's categories to festival voices tells how the textual conception and the play conception are locked together visually. Instead of seeing a text before us, we see playing all around us and desire to assert that it is the **real** festival and not the festival as a reading of a text. Interpretation and play form a false visual opposition that can all too easily comprehend a festival whole: normative versus orectic poles (Turner 1982) ritual versus play (Manning 1983).

Dutch medievalist Johan Huizinga, in his book *Homo Ludens* (1955), enunciated this "commonsense" opposition of text to play in its most fundamental form when he defined play as a 'free activity' standing quite consciously outside 'ordinary life' as being 'not serious.' But Huizinga, no doubt an heir of Alpers' descriptive painters, cannily included the observation that play also has its rules. While students of festivals, like festival-goers, have been finding oppositions between the text side and the play side of the festival, students of play, following Huizinga, have long since invented an autonomous theory which locates both text and play within a larger concept of play. The game, with its rules and competition, is the text set against the free activity of play.

Psychologists Jean Piaget (1951) and Erik Erikson (1950) have each in his way made use of the game / pure play distinction in stage theories of child development: the free form play of toddlers and preschool children passes into the structured, antagonistic games of school children and young adults. A sequence of play types culminates in the socialization of the growing individual, which is a passage from play to textuality. Roger Caillois (1961) planted two poles (Greek and Latin), *paidea* (free play) versus *ludus* (games) and set up four Greek columns alongside their field, refining the internal distinctions of the play subject yet further. In this Olympic field, culture evolves from childish *paidea* to mannerly *ludus* through an increasing presence of the orderly elements of competition *(agon)* and chance-play *(alea),* much as the Piagetian or the Eriksonian child becomes a functioning adult as it moves through stages of play. Gazing upon Caillois' map with favor, Turner (1983:109–10) deplores the positivistic downgrading of the primitive and chastises Caillois with sound anthropological primitivism.

Caillois' formulation, however, reveals what is beneath this theory of play from Huizinga onward: Nietzsche's Dionysian / Apollonian phases. Free play tends strongly to develop a dialectical relationship with games corresponding to the free Dionysian and the ordered Apollonian strains in playing. This may explain Turner's career-long quest for credible pairs of concepts.

An anecdote of Ibsen tells of his keeping a portrait of Strindberg, whom he despised, hanging over his writing desk. Asked why, he answered, "Because I cannot write a line without that madman staring down at me." A contemporary anthropologist might say the same of Nietzsche, for whom the Dionysian was "compared to the Apollonian, the eternal and artistic power that first calls the whole world of phenomena into existence . . ." (Nietzche 1967:143). The flat logic of the Apollonian (the preferred anthropological usage since Ruth Benedict) gives way to the eruptive force of the Dionysian, which then is succeeded by a reassertion of the Apollonian. In any one moment the two are, as Nietzsche says, "interwoven," and their relations in a work or a writer are most subtle. Nietzsche's Euripides, Alpers' Velazquez and Victor Turner's

Brazilian *Carnaval* exhibit this subtle intertwining of Apollonian and Dionysian, iconic and descriptive modes, *paidea* and *ludus*. The only way to hear the festival voice of play is to return the subject to Nietzsche, and instead of trying to separate play from the festival text (or game), to wrap it together with the text in one frenzied act—the carnival, the festival, or whatever celebratory term is preferred.

Turner (1969) himself patented a term for this twist from play to game and round again: he called it communitas and he was sure to use it whenever he turned his hand to describing a festival. Turner, of course, took communitas to mean a great deal more than this. I am convinced, however, that the term is intended to state the Nietzschean problematic of festival play. Turner occasionally lapses into plain characteristics, even stages, of play—as in his liminal/liminoid dichotomy (1977). But for the most part, he keeps a faith in the redemptive (that is precisely the word) entwining energy of communitas (1969:131–65, read carefully). Reading the state of communitas (in carnivals and campus uprisings) as a restoration of true play to a game-weary world, theologian Harvey Cox (1969) finds it the sort of socialized redemption badly needed today and makes communitas stagnantly Apollonian. Turner himself was quick to point out how easily this happens.

The word play has in English (as have its equivalents in other languages, *spiel* in German, *jeu* in French) semantic resonances that bring drama (and music) to its voice. This is also in keeping with Nietzsche's and Turner's concerns: the history of drama as the history of culture and the dramatistic study of culture. Euripides seated the spectator on the stage ". . . the mirror in which formerly only grand and bold traits were represented now showed the painful fidelity that conscientiously reproduces even the botched outlines of nature" (Nietzsche 1967:77). And Turner, with a bow to Weber as well as Nietzsche, placed communitas within structure (1969:132–33), showing that communitas tended to become "routinized" and normative. Both Nietzsche and Turner found the play in this inclusion, the drama arising not out of simple existence of tragedy or of communitas but out of the confrontation between Dionysian communitas and Apollonian spectatorship. Communitas is unwatched and participatory; structure is watched and exclusive.

Paidea and *ludus*, free play and game correspond to this dramatistic opposition, and all converge in play.

Critics of Turner's work, such as Boon (1982), mistake Turner's intent when they accuse him of "implying a collapse of structure rather than an additional articulation of structure." Turner's drama of culture, and play of culture, are dialectical articulations of structure with anti-structure. Turner was Nietzsche's spectator allowed to sit upon the stage and know he is part of the tragedy. The whole—the drama and its spectator playing together—is the performance.

The "deep play" (again a pun) of the Balinese cockfight is a performance—"an example, carefully prepared," and not an imitation or a depiction, says Geertz (1972:446). But I think he must mean an exemplum, a moral performance. Javanese proletarian dramas are "rites of modernization" (Peacock 1968), because they include the spectators in a cultural performance that is far larger than the theatre pieces they watch. And the Ramlila of Ramnagar (drama, festival and spectacle, is a performance "bringing thousands of spectators into a celebratory time-space: a time-space in which the mythic rulers of legendary days, played by ordinary people, contain the actual rulers of today" (Schechner 1982:93).

These are all what Kenneth Burke (1945:323) calls "matters of substance and enactment, a dialectic of constitutions." Evoking Burke casts us away from the charmed harbor where the play voice plays. The pun of this entire section is suddenly gone. Sutton-Smith (1980:18–19) offers to solve the Nietzschean play/game dialectic with a sociolinguistic theory linking communications with drama, in which performance separates itself from script. In Schechner's performance theory (1977) script has an evolutionary relationship with performance itself, just as Caillois' *ludus* evolves from *paidea*, and the text returns full-fledged and absolute: Schechner will not even distinguish between "a genuine ritual" and "a fabricated one" (Bharucha 1984:16). Folk festivals inspired Shakespeare to compose his immortal texts (Barber 1959). The festival voice of play is lost in writing just as it seems to have emerged most boldly.

Festival as Release

Festival play is fully in force only when its voice becomes a cry. Then the dyadic or dialectic interplay of text, game and script ceases. The pent-up emotion erupts; its explosion dominates the festival.

Aristotle's definition of tragedy in the *Poetics* (vi.2) includes a provision for the drama "through pity and fear effecting the proper *katharsis*, or purgation, of these emotions." S.H. Butcher, examining Aristotle's reflections on catharsis, derives an account of how tragedy functions cathartically: "Pity and fear are purged of the impure element which clings to them in life. In the glow of tragic excitement these feelings are so transformed that the net result is a noble emotional satisfaction" (1951:267). Catharsis, which is analogous to medical purgation, exercises a morally uplifting influence upon the spectator. Tragedy "acts on the feelings, not on the will. It does not make men better, but it removes certain hindrances to virtue" (p.269).

Manuel, a Bolivian miner whom June Nash interviewed in 1970, spoke of Carnival as Aristotle spoke of tragedy:

> Carnival is a pause, a rest, a spiritual release, a moral flushing-out, an escape, a liberation, a form of expressing one's sorrow and at the same time one's joy. You must understand that the miners work the year round in the mine, and sometimes when they want to have freedom to make a fiesta, to dance in a team, to make a ch'alla, they cannot do it. And so they wait until the fiesta of Carnival, when they give vent to all these pent-up desires (1979:126).

Aristotle was much less ready than his master Plato to condemn "popular amusements" and was "more aware of the plurality of approximate ends that charming and moving performances might serve" (Gilbert and Kuhn 1972:81–82). The experience of the Greek philosopher and of the Bolivian *cholo* intersect at least on the common ground of festival. Both scholars and festival-goers (admittedly coincident populations) voice release and play theories of festival.

The Carnival that the Bolivian miner describes is cathartic in the most Aristotelian sense, but it promises another kind of release which Aristotle never intended. The miners' restrained wish to celebrate can be fulfilled only during the privileged period of Carnival. The language which Manuel uses is universally appreciable: the desire to dance and play builds up as a kind of internal pressure escaping on the occasion of Carnival. Tragedy's catharsis sets straight moral life by drawing the spectator into the performance. It is a response to an outside presentation. Carnival's pressure release is a voiding of what has become impossible to contain much longer. No wonder Nash, who is committed to a Marxist interpretation of the *cholos'* culture, ignores half of what Manuel told her to concentrate on: the cathartic solidarity-achieving power of Carnival.

The hydraulic or steam-pressure image of human emotion has an ancient and wide circulation. In a context of digression, it would be pleasant to discuss the Hindu concept of *tapas*, the Chinese *chi*, the East African "hot / cool" and their explanation of occasions of release. An Anglo-American reader can easily relate to the vernacular of "getting hot under the collar" and "letting off steam." Applied to an entire society this pressure-release opinion is a ready explanation for festival behavior. The festival is an occasion for and of mass depressurizing.

It appeals to many readers to hear that a festival is a pressure release. Anthropologists and folklorists are susceptible to such a simple characterization. But most trained observers prefer to make a slight semantic shift and term the festival a "safety valve" preserving the whole social steam jacket by allowing release in one place. The theory of ritual, in general, provides for occasional displays of disorder in the interest of reaffirming the overall order. Order is the object. The more violent the release, the more powerful it is in returning the entire society to a state of normalcy.

The Zulu "rites of rebellion" observed by Gluckman (1963) could alleviate internal antagonisms between ruler and groups of subjects by acting out revolts. This style of release, Gluckman warns, is only possible where no one questions the firmness of the social order that permits the rites. Likewise, the Hindu festival of Holi surprises even the anthropologist (Marriott 1966) with its disruption, but ultimately it teaches everyone "to play his routine roles afresh."

Thus, anthropologists carefully grounded the issuing steam in an Aristotelian Catharsis. The irrational and destructive release is to the greater good of the entire society. In fact, the moment of release is a stepping outside the usual frame into a special place set aside for the manifestation of these unseemly forces. The "orthodox Durkheimian sociology" prescribes a line of time with shifts "from the Normal-Profane order of existence into the Abnormal-Sacred order and back again" (Leach 1961:134). Quoting T.S. Eliot, Turner (1984:4), refers to ritual performance as "this moment in and out of time". With a sigh of relief, the anthropologist says that these celebrations, even when they return violent, are liminal to the functioning social order and imply that they require an order to which to be liminal.

The anthropological version of festival release, from Durkheim through Evans-Pritchard and Leach to Gluckman and Turner, is an Aristotelian Catharsis for the health of the social order.

The catharsis might not be healthy at all, but a symptom of the sickness. The buildup of steam in Freudian theory is the libido continually denied the very material gratificatiions it must enjoy. The denial is repression, one cathexis or deferral of libidinous desires; the "release" of the repressed desires is, however, also a cathexis, sublimation, also a deferral of genuine gratification. The early Freud saw hope in the rationalization of the cathexes through analysis. The pleasure principle (eros) dominated libidinous wishes and presented the chance of rectification as it had contributed to the formation of neuroses. After the First World War, Freud increasingly judged civilization itself a sickness and replaced eros with thanatos, the death principle. The aim of human action was not self-gratification but self-immolation. Though Freud did not live to see the fiery end of the Second World War, he was enough singed by the Holocaust to feel confirmed in his beliefs.

The two strains in Freudian thought, both of which have undergone considerable development and hybridization, sound tones in the festival voice of release. The pleasure principle is adaptable to the Aristotelian and Durkheimian approaches if some of Freud's stipulations are ignored. Gluckman makes the case for Turner:

> According to Turner, what the ritual symbol does, is to effect 'an interchange of qualities between its (ideological and sensory) poles of meaning. Norms and values, on the one hand become saturated with emotion, while the gross and base emotions become ennobled through contact with social values. The irksomeness of moral constraint is transformed into the "love of goodness". The thesis obviously 'fits' with the Freudian theory of sublimation—but it states a social process (1965:292–93).

Gluckman quotes this passage from Turner's ruminations over

Ndembu symbolism to evidence the fit with Freud; yet the passage is, referring to the transformation of irksomeness of restraint into moral goodness, also an evocation of Aristotelian catharsis. Achieving "love of goodness" is indeed a sublimation, but even the early Freud would have seen some irony in saying this.

Turner formed his theory of "normative" and "orectic" poles of festival (in general ritual) symbolism in his Ndembu writings and defended the pairing. This dynamic typology fulfils the orderly wishes of his functionalist predecessors and makes an allowance for outpourings of festive emotion. The normative drive into the orectic stablizes the normative. The ugly, inconvenient but important items of the orectic pole (blood, semen, rejoicing, devouring), stand in a good relation with the institutional, structural normative when they are off on the side, sublime and temporary.

This model, ever Freudian / Aristotelian, supports a large literature in anthropology and psychiatry on the therapeutic value of ritual and festival. The social and moral goodness is also personal goodness. The ceremonies of the Moroccan Islamic brotherhood, the Hamadsha, are therapeutic procedures that "move an individual from a state of illness to a state of health" (Crapanzano 1973:212). The equally violent Gisaro ceremony of the Kaluli is individually and socially curative, a thing of beauty and an expression of social process (Schieffelin 1976:222-23).

The Freudian doctrine of sublimation, however, would be amenable to the Aristotelian usages of anthropology only if it could yield an order, however temporary. Brown (1959:137-38) contends that the concept of sublimation contradicts the absolute separation between nature and culture that anthropologists favor, setting up an ambiguity that Freud himself was hard-pressed to encompass when he put his hand to cultural analysis. High and refined as the accomplishments of a Leonardo da Vinci might be, they are still the results of sublimation. How much moreso the poorer sublimations of the masses; how much more of the animal nature their efforts at sublimation must display. If the festival is sublimation then it is not a particularly effective or elevated sublimation. A hierarchy of sublimations arises. The anthropologists' festival, to be sublimation at all, must be exalted sublimation. It must be orderly; it must be art. The stink and the copulation can be there, yet only if they become in the end the sweet smell of success and the prosperous issue of family life. Only the pleasure principle, and an expurgated form of it, makes for festival release.

The therapeutic interpretation of festivity suits the pleasure principle well, and has the additional advantage of making festivity 'useful'. Another large category of ethnographic examples makes festive sublimation yet more concrete and utilitarian: drug-induced release. Tobacco, alcohol and other more dramatically hallucinogenic substances figure in worship and celebration throughout the world. The strength of the pleasure principle in anthropological research can be measured by the ethnographers' need to feel that consumption of the drugs accomplishes an ultimate social good, whether it be integation of the drug-taker into the society or the rectification of community. The more sober writings on the ritual use of hallucinogens, such as those collected by Furst (1972), all emphasize the hardships accompanying the consumption of drugs, but justify them in the net gains for the society and individual from this single potent experience.

The ambiguity of the sublimation achieved is seldom noted. Furst concludes his argument with the statement that his chief informant, Ramon Medina Silva, an artist and a shaman of the Huichol peyote religion, died from wounds he received in a shooting incident at his *rancho*. There was a fiesta to celebrate the planting of the first maize crop and a great deal of drinking, which, Furst implies, led to abandon and the shooting. Peyote was of course not involved. Furst never pauses to consider that the ritual sublimity of peyote might in some way correspond to the festive depravity of alcohol, that these are two aspects of the same ambiguous sublimation, and that Ramon, whose sensitivity and artistry is clear from Furst's and from Myerhoff's account (1977), was nonetheless a festival-maker, a consumer and victim of alcohol.

Freud's treatment of war-crazed soldiers may have led him to conceive of thanatos, the death urge, which eventually overcame the pleasure principle in his writings (e.g., *Beyond the Pleasure Principle*). Certainly the First World War was destruction and mayhem more vast and slow than even very perverse sublimation would dictate. As joyous, healing, liberating, and morally corrective as festivals might be, as much as sublimation can be channeled into catharsis for the greater sociocultural good, there remains in the festival a destructive element that exceeds release. Catharsis and sublimation are most fundamentally ambiguous: the possibility of black murderous rage is also a part of the festival. That tone in the voice is most frantically suppressed by both participants and theorists, because it rules completely when it emerges fully.

The huge vehicle of the Lord Jagannatha, a form of the deity Krishna, moves through streets of Puri in Orissa, crowded with votaries on festival day, crushing anyone who happens to fall beneath its wheels. On Puram in Trichur, Kerala, two ranks of fifteen elephants converge down the main boulevard with similar results for anyone caught between them. Carnivals in Europe and the New World are expected to have their casualties. In traditional China, the Midsummer Festival on the Double Fifth, the fifth day of the fifth month, was celebrated with Dragon Boat races, sometimes leading to battles and deaths that amounted to human sacrifices (Bodde 175:314–15). Death is rife at mass celebrations, but it is always considered either an accidental deviation from the festival's sublime purpose or the residue of some primitive human sacrifice lingering half-forgotten on the festival's periphery. A thanatos, a positive drive toward killing, cannot be allowed.

Festivals turned bloody are for historians, who can treat them as particularly significant departures from the normal good time. Ladurie (1979) makes a profound social text out of one sixteenth-century carnival performance by this method, and Canetti (1984) contemplates the murderous push in festivals in terms more general than the local and the historical. In the "religions of lament," for instance, Canetti discerns the pack's emotional identification with the victim:

> Why is it that so many join the lament? What is its attraction? What does it give people? To all those who join it the same thing happens: the hunting and baiting pack expiates its guilt by becoming a lamenting pack. Men lived as pursuers and as such, in their own fashion, they continue to live. They seek alien flesh, and cut into it, feeding on the torment of weaker creatures; the glazing eye of the victim is mirrored in their eyes, and that last cry they delight in is indelibly recorded in their soul. Most of them perhaps do not divine that, while they feed their bodies, they also feed the darkness within themselves (1984:145).

Canetti proposes a theory of group thanatos that more than counterbalances the group eros (catharsis, sublimation) of the anthropologists. Murder, or the spectacle of death not prevented, does not (as the more cynical sublimationists might provide) improve the group or the individual; it only feeds the darkness within.

Festival as Inversion

The heaps of dead are exactly the opposite of the wildly moving folk usually depicted at a festival. The death urge is much easier to handle if it seems another festival inversion, if the voice of inversion sounds over the lament of death or the cry of release.

Inversions are the most readily documented festival behavior: the man become woman, and woman become man; the human become animal; the high and clean become low and dirty. Frazer in *The Golden Bough* (1919:306–411) wrote of the social inversions that occurred at the time of Roman Saturnalia, European Carnival, and comparable Asian festivals. Though he perceived the pervasiveness of the Saturnalia type of festival and took it as evidence of the homogeneity of ancient civilization across Asia into Europe, he preferred to emphasize the festival as the time of a sacred or divine king's rule degenerating with time into Lord of Misrule and effigy-burning traditions. Frazer placed the inversions on a historical continuum with old agricultural rites, isolating them in an evolutionary corridor. He recognized that they are "outbursts of the pent-up forces of human nature, too often degenerating into wild orgies of lust and crime . . ."(306). But, as Hyman (1962) has made clear, Frazer, while having similar interests, did not sympathize with Freud. Although Freud was strongly influenced by Frazer and sent him his work for approval, Frazer would not even read it. The inversions were signs of a historical process, not of individual passions. Frazer alluded disapprovingly to the outbursts of disorder without wanting to discuss them. Casting aside dangerous inversions is a pattern in anthropological discussion of festivals: recall Furst's and Myerhoff's failure to take full account of the death, and therefore the life, of their informant Ramon.

Inversion pleases analysts as long as it remains structural in nature. It fits comfortably into schemes such as Leach's, as a movement from the profane toward the sacred, and such as Turner's, as a symbolism of anti-structure and liminality. Declaring that a man dressing as a woman, or a peasant acting the landlord are inversions presupposes a knowledge of an uninverted exterior. Without this knowledge, labeling a festival behavior "inversion" begs the question on a cultural scale. The answer already exists in the question asked, "What is this an inversion of?" The knowledge required, the social system or the normal way of life, then takes shape accordingly.

Bauman and Abrahams (1978:193-208) go a long way toward exposing the naivete of such judgments. They establish the relationship between the "functionalist argument in the interpretation of rites of reversal" and the "safety-value" mechanism, "by which the pressures engendered by social conflict may be vented without allowing the conflict to become fully overt and threaten the survival of the society." Their examples of St. Vincent Carnival and Nova Scotia belsnickling however, show, that the apparent reversal and disorder of these occasions are not their main organizing principles. Disorder and licence exist year-round in these communities, and commonly encounter order and respectability in scenes of confusion. At festival time this confrontation is a convergence. "The picture is not one of hostility, but of harmony." The writers conclude that "People have a greater tolerance for disorder than anthropologists give them credit for, and analysis of festivals of symbolic inversion must take account of the place of this disorder in their lives."

While the conclusion substitutes one form of naivete for another—the belief in ultimate harmony for the belief in immediate disorder—the point that festival inversion must be compared with what it is supposedly inverting is well taken. If disorderly behavior, and the actions termed inversions can be documented in the run of behavior outside festival precincts, then they are not special to the festival and do not set it off so strictly from the rest of the world. Frazer based his assumption that Saturnalia involved inversion on the statements of classical authors; he did not inquire into the social history of master-servant relations in ancient Rome. Had he done so he may have claimed that "inversions" were more a part of everyday life than his aristocratic informants wanted to believe. The same might be said of master-peasant relations in Europe, the New World, and Asia. Frazer portrayed the social order to which he was committed by installing its opposite within the festival.

The same is true of Bauman and Abrahams, although they are

several steps removed from Frazer. They reject inversion as the internal characteristic of festivals, only to predicate upon the festivals a grander, more positive, inversion. Festival harmony takes the place of everyday disharmony. Bauman and Abrahams invert the priorities of functionalist theory, and their explicit theory returns to Frazer's implicit assumptions. The whole ends harmoniously, socially and/or historically.

Inversion is a voice necessary to festivals. Whether what takes place in a festival is in truth the reverse of what normally happens, people need to think so. Here again the analysts show themselves to be festival participants sounding one voice more loudly than the others. Inversion is one of those autonomous, tautological assertions that foster a world inside and out. Occasions are festivals because people think they are times of inversion and try to make what they think (and have long thought) is inversion happen during those times. The voice of inversion does not describe anything outside of the moment of its utterance. The master become slave and vice versa in a festival satisfies some, because the 'change' implies the existence of normality outside, when in fact the only normality is the festival itself read as an inversion. There is no pure, incontestable inversion, although some festival-goers rejoice in thinking so.

Elite communities of interpreters, anthropologists, folklorists, and historians like to invoke the cliché of inversion to assure themselves that there is order in the world—and to give the impression that they have insight into the mentality of the festival-goers. After all, they (or we) are part of the Establishment and have the most to lose if things are turned upside down, and the most to gain if we can be convinced that our state is the opposite of something clearly degraded. Celebrating inversion is a positional catharsis for elites who appreciate how little they have to lose by pretending to lose it all. Inversion is "playing chicken" with an identity guaranteed by the narrative voice.

Marriott (1966) tells with laudable candor how he passed Holi in a North Indian village, first hiding from the revellers, then "made to dance in the streets, fluting like Lord Krishna, with a garland of old shoes around my neck"—the opposite of his staid usual role. One wonders how other anthropologists living in Indian villages were able to avoid this treatment. One knows why they avoid describing it. Yet Marriott himself saw only the irony of inversion from the elevated standpoint to which he returned to write his account. It is fully conceivable that people at the festival saw no inversion at all in his behavior, not even a symbolic change. What they did see is problematic.

Inversion is a habit of conceiving, which the position of the elite interpreter compels us to assume, whether or not it is 'really' found in the festival and is important to the experience. An inversion interpretation overlays Lincoln's analysis (1985) of revolutionary exhumations of Catholic clerics at the outbreak of the Spanish Civil War in July 1936. Lincoln does not employ "inversion," but describes the revolution itself as a series of inversions, and comparing the exhumations to other "rituals of collective obscenity" he brings them into line with numerous anthropological and historical examples. He is so intent on establishing the desire of the revolutionaries to invert the sanctity of the Catholic Church that he does not investigate Spanish festival usages or the folklore of corpses in Spain, which might show the exhumations to be less revolutionary than they seem. Lincoln's own disgust at the phenomenon and determination to make sense of the event, in addition to the interpretive biases of his community, edged him toward conceiving an inversion without examining the immediate cultural context.

Interpreters and participants, hearing the voice of inversion in festivals and revolutions, know only what they require to keep the festivities in motion.

Conclusion: The Voice of Closure

Festivals, and speculation about them, manage to be over and done with. Festivals are delimited in time and space. They are subject to a poetic closure which prevents them, if they are to remain festivals, from spilling over into the other departments of life. This voice is a restraining authority. It may actually be embodied in figures who watch over the festival and control it on behalf of power whose interests must be protected. The police have a role in all festivals. That they are seldom remarked on is a testament to their effectiveness in exercising unobtrusive control. And to the complicity of the commentator.

The voice of closure is in the festival itself, modulating its cultural shape. Eating and drinking to excess, typical of festivals, are decisively, enjoyably, finite while seeming infinite. There is only so much food or drink anyone can consume before the festival is over. Sex, contests and gambling, also officially or unofficially common in festivals, are much the same. The festival culminates in satiety, exhaustion, bankruptcy, success or, for a few, death. Festival metaphors may be open-ended, but festival action is closed. It must stop. So must theorizing.

CHAPTER **2**

Chorus

From the polyphony of festival theory to the polyphony of the St. Peter's Fiesta is but a small skip. Let us listen to the chorus and try to hear the many voices of this sonorous tradition.

The Atlantic

The settlers of Gloucester—English, Finnish, Portuguese, and Italian— crossed the ocean and extracted their living from it. The Atlantic Ocean is the constant unremembered voice of the fiesta. It sounds unremittingly, relentlessly throughout all activities of the fiesta. The fiesta celebrates the ocean, and the ocean is to the fiesta as sound is to music—necessary, unnoticed.

Gloucester

The town and subsequent city of Gloucester contributes its own voice. It has long since become a carefully enunciated monody. In 1623-24, the Dorchester Company sent a group from England to start a fishing settlement in the Gloucester harbor. However, their salt plant burned down, and the weather was unbearable. Discouraged, they returned to England, or moved to Salem. A permanent colony established itself in the harbor in 1642, under the leadership of a dissident minister from the Massachusetts Bay Colony, whose followers were driven by fishing and the wish for religious independence. Fishing, always more important than the maritime trade that brought wealth to towns further up and down the coast, did make Gloucester prosperous. In time, the prosperity led to the sharpening of economic classes, the construction of residences to display class standing, and eventually the writing of history.

History began and ended in Gloucester around 1860. That voice started up among old families dislocated by the collapse of the economic system which had enriched Gloucester. Cod caught by Gloucester boats was salted and loaded in Boston, Marblehead, or Salem for sale in Spain or Portugal in exchange for molasses, which in turn bought slaves in Africa who in turn were sold to planters in Spanish America, Surinam, or the Caribbean Islands. However, the British Royal Navy's campaign against slavery slowly erased the bottom line of this Golden Triangle. Fishing was still profitable but not so profitable.

In 1860, John J. Babson published *A History of the Town of Gloucester, Cape Ann*, a ponderous volume of family chronicles and impressive buildings. Babson's book resembles the local histories a number of New England towns of like age were generating during the late nineteenth century. In Babson's history, fishing itself is less important than the social life, which was not unlike that found anywhere in New England. The book immortalized the milieu of its own creation.

Around the same time there developed in the same milieu institutions designed to preserve the traces of that social world. The Gloucester Lyceum, a lecture group founded in 1830, gradually assembled a library and found a patron in Dr. Samuel Sawyer, who gave it funds, his name, and finally his house (1884), which became the Glolucester Lyceum and Sawyer Free Library, today still privately owned though accessible to the public. In 1872, the Cape Ann Historical Association grew out of the lyceum, and eventually acquired a house, a Paul Revere silver service, and a splendid gallery of paintings by the Gloucester maritime painter Fitz Hugh Lane (1804–65). The staff of these institutions maintain a genealogical connection with the Gloucester past, as well as collections of genealogical literature. The mystical communication of blood through the generations assures this continuity in the librarians of today, whose families have always been in Gloucester, who know every detail of the city's history but who, when first asked, had never heard of an Italian-American fiesta.

In 1864, one of those fires that slip so easily through wooden New England towns in winter obliterated a large part of Gloucester's Main Street. The shape of the old buildings was retained in daguerreotype mercury and on salted paper long after the buildings were rebuilt and the shape of the streets altered. The photos made their way through attics and collections, joining diaries, family documents, discrete nautical memorabilia, and furniture to form the nucleus of the collection today housed in the Cape Ann Historical Society.

Houses that survived lent names to this growing historical voice. The Sargent-Murray-Gilman-Hough house on Main Street is an architectural genealogy and a monument to American Universalism, the Murray part of the name being Rev. John Murray, who brought the doctrine to Gloucester in 1779. Houses with names or with signs that date them (circa) at a respectable distance from the present are inviolable: any attempt to destroy or alter them raises a cry of protest from the community. When the 1970s urban renewal of the downtown area threatened some ancient residences, the forces of renewal had to make concessions to the armed preservers of old Gloucester.

However, named houses were vulnerable if they did not recite history canonically. During the summer of 1970 I watched a large, ornate Victorian mansion fall under the wrecker's ball. Its owner had appealed to the city and then to private parties to move the house off the land rather than have it demolished; no one responded. The house site was needed for a new museum of Gloucester history. A local historian explained to me that the sea captain who had built the house during the late 1870's was an "arriviste" (not of old family) who had disgraced the downtown with the conspicuous extravagance of his house's ornamentation. I watched the ball smash wooden scrolls, pediments, lancet windows, and a massive door which would have brought a sizeable sum on the restoration market. The captain could not buy his way into Gloucester history with an outlay of cash; every particle of his pretence was wiped away.

The Babson cottage on the Gloucester-Rockport Road remained standing, dated, named and signposted because the family that had settled there produced John J. Babson, the local historian and Roger Babson, the financier and founder of Babson College. Roger Babson used his wealth to imprint his family name and his philosophy upon Gloucester: the Isabel Babson Memorial Library on Main Street honors an ancestral midwife who settled on that spot by loaning books to expectant mothers; the house at 58 Middle Street, where Babson was born, is now the headquarters of the Open Church

Foundation, dedicated to keeping churches open all the time; and Dogtown Common, the eerie abandoned pariah village in the center of Cape Ann, bears pithy messages Babson had carved on its rocks. Babson set in stone what others set on paper.

In August, 1923, on the 300th anniversary of the first settlement in Gloucester, the town staged a pageant-drama, what Pringle (1923) called a "picturization" of "New England's oldest fishing town." In the pamphlet published to accompany the production, Pringle did not stress the historical quality of the events depicted, but by drama sought to render live the events among which Gloucester people (of his elite community) dwelt. The pageant began with the arrival of the Norsemen, and proceeded in a series of separate episodes: the landing of Champlain in 1606; Captain John Smith's visit in 1614; the Dorchester expedition's departure and arrival, 1623; the 1745 Gloucester participation in the British attack on the French fort of Louisburg, Nova Scotia; the revolutionary era; and the Civil War.

The pageant ended where history stopped, in the 1860s. It was performed on the wide open space of Stage Fort Park by a cast of hundreds. The participants, listed in Pringle's pamphlet, were mostly English and Scots-Irish; exceptions included a few Finns who played the Norsemen, and two Portuguese. Italian names are conspicuously absent. Nor is there any mention of a Portuguese or Italian presence in Gloucester history, which had started to present itself at the Civil War.

The 350th anniversary celebration of Gloucester in 1973 had no pageant, but several days of plays and performances, which referred to the same pre-Civil War history and not to subsequent events. There was one significant difference between the celebrations of 1923 and 1973: in 1973 the pageant committee had two Italian names. Gloucester's history still ended in the 1860s, although inherited by a new community. Those wishing to act upon Gloucester history have that history flat and legible before them. Events in Gloucester since history ended have their stage elsewhere.

Fishermen

The Gloucester tricentennial celebration in 1923 included the erection of a monument to the chief occupation and livelihood of its men, fishing. After considerable local debate, the monument became a metal statue of a gale-blown fisherman standing at the wheel, which soon became a local attraction. It has always been in Gloucester's interest to sweeten and soften the social, political, economic, and olfactory realities of the trade with statues and celebrations of fishing. At the same time, the statue is a symbolic conjunction between Gloucester's oldest trade and the newer trade of art-making.

Cod, being a groundfish, spends its life after hatching on the ocean floor in water from twenty to well over a thousand feet deep (Jensen 1972). The fry hatch from eggs spawned on the surface and after about two months begin a long descent, gradually acclimatizing themselves to the increasing pressure as they sink. Adult cod eat other fish, squid, and molluscs, which abound in their zone of water. Fishing captains could always tell good cod grounds from the coarse sand and broken shells adhering to a waxed leaden bob dropped to the ocean floor.

To take advantage of the vast numbers of cod congregated on the Grand Banks off the American northeast coast, New England fishermen early developed setline fishing (Meltzer 1980:20–22). A series of hooks baited with squid (the cod's favorite food) was strung on a solid line, perhaps thousands of feet long, and set out in the water by men in small boats called dories. The lines had to be laid carefully to prevent currents from fouling them and to keep worthless fish closer to the surface from taking the bait. A set of small barrel floats kept the line on the surface while the hooks snagged the fish. After a time the fishermen would carefully draw up a section of the line, slit the throats of the thrashing fish and swing them into the prow of the boat, all without touching fish or hook with the bare hand. The line was rebaited as cod, dogfish, halibut, and others were removed. On board the mother ship, the men systematically removed the liver (kept for making codliver oil) and gutted, boned, salted, and stacked the fish in the hold. The suitability of cod to salting—few other fish keep so well if properly treated—is what made cod fishing into an industry of transatlantic importance. During its first year of existence alone, Massachusetts Bay Colony was able to ship 300,000 cod to England. The remarkable economic versatility of the cod encouraged several subsidiary industries. "Cape Cod girls they have no combs/they comb their hair with codfish bones," sang deepwater sailors. For years, a wooden cod hanging in the Massachusetts State Legislature recalled the commonwealth's chief product, and perhaps its flavor.

The common dory fisherman laid out line for hours, landed fish for hours and salted fish for hours more (see Bartlett 1977). The dangers of his life were dull dangers: a fog might develop, separating him from the mother schooner and he might never see safety again through the soup; or a tired knife stroke might take a joint of a finger rather than the cod's gut. The folklore of the fisheries was full of survival (or nonsurvival) stories: the doryman who made it to land or to another ship through storm or fog; the dory found mysteriously adrift and unmanned on the Banks. Howard Blackburn, out in a dory and separated from the schooner during a gale in 1883, rowed for five days without food or water before he was rescued. He lost all his fingers, but still managed to keep a saloon in Gloucester and sail sloops unaided twice across the Atlantic. Blackburn was one fisherman who left his name around the town, but he was only one.

Not all fishermen were captains, though the captains were and are taken to represent all fishermen. The social system of the fishermen was like their existence in general—quite static. A fishing boat was a highly capitalized enterprise that had to bring in a considerable catch to turn a profit. It never brought the windfalls of the merchant voyages. The line of advancement from cabin boy to captain and then to respectable patriarch was a credible fable in merchant shipping but a fantasy for most fishermen.

Because fishing expeditions were brief compared to whaling or trading trips, Gloucester never was a sailortown like New Bedford or Salem. The voice of fishing is the captains' voice; it speaks in museums, monuments, and libraries. The fishermen's monument is a captain at the wheel guiding the metaphoric ship of state and not the common fisherman fogbound in a dory. The voice of the captains should not be mistaken for the voice of the fishermen.

The voice of the fishermen is very hard to hear. It is easy to invent the voice out of vicarious sympathy with the conditions of their labor. Being illiterate, the fishermen themselves left little record: illiteracy itself has the character of a statement. In Gloucester the common fishermen were a social and economic underclass remaining in place and scarcely changing over the years. The sound of the doryman's conch through the fog is a voice heard faintly through the many books written on Gloucester fishermen and fisheries. These writings began to appear about the same time as the first town histories. James G. Procter was especially determined to make this voice heard. His *Fishermen's Memorial and Record Book* (1873) was followed by *Fishermen's Ballads and Songs of the Sea* (1874) written with his brother, and *The Fishermen's Own Book* (1882). These efforts to make the fishermen's voice more audible actually succeeded in establishing a romantic literary image of the Gloucester fishermen, which has persisted in its own autonomous tradition. James B. Connolly wrote a large number of novels (e.g., *Seiners*, 1904; *Gloucestermen*, 1930) and some popular nonfiction all of which dramatized the fantasy of the tough, brave, all-enduring fishermen. Procter and Connolly have a number of successors, including journalists such as Geoffrey Moorehouse, who sign on a fishing boat for a brief time and write a book on the fishermen's experience that carries forward the old image with few changes. The common fisherman became a closed text around the same time that the history of Gloucester did.

The fishermen themselves have become ghosts. A ballad published in Gloucester late in the nineteenth century, *The Ghostly Fishermen*, tells of a ghost crew who mounted the deck of the vessel that had earlier rammed and sunk their schooner. The ballad acquired a tune and passed up the coast as far as Newfoundland. Although it is a pleasant song to hear at folk festivals, it does not carry the voice of the fishermen: it recalls how dim that voice has become next to the literate voice of the captains. As always the fishermen are passive: they melt into the fog, leaving only a trace of guilt rapidly redeemed in statues and films which blanket their side of the endeavor.

The fisherman's job could be occupied by anyone able to perform the tasks, but because of the skill required some knowledge of fishing was preferable. Immigrants were often among the early fishermen. Irish, Finns and Portuguese were the first foreign groups to enter the Gloucester cod fishery in any numbers. Whaling captains, who always lost crew through desertions, picked up men in the Azores and carried them back to New England where they quit whaling for the steadier employment of the fishing fleet. The Portuguese came in numbers sufficient to found a distinct settlement on the hilly slopes a distance from the main town. They formed a separate Catholic parish in 1889 and three years later constructed their own church.

Changing conditions in the fishing industry made it possible for Portuguese to become masters of a small number of schooners.

The changes were technological and then social. American Grand Banks fishermen borrowed the practice of gill-netting from the Norwegians in the late 1870s. During the spawning season, when cod come to the surface and refuse to take bait, a net dragged through a school of fish snag their gills and yield a large catch with little labor other than holding and hauling in the net. This method was restricted to the spawning season. It took fishermen little time to realize that during other seasons of the year they could drag a net over the cod's home territory on the bed of the ocean. The design of the nets grew more sophisticated too. The shape of the opening and the bag was made suitable for the sea floor. Thus a minimum amount of energy was required to bring in a maximum number of fish.

A simple change in preservation technology also altered conditions. In 1905 some captains began to preserve their fish in ice flakes instead of salt. Ice preservation simultaneously improved the flavor of the fish and encouraged the development of the haddock fishery, since haddock, better tasting and easier to catch than cod, kept well in ice (but not in salt). Ice helped augment the catch yet further. In 1898 the total catch of all Gloucester fisheries was 100 million pounds; by 1906 it was 150 million pounds. The same technology persisted and the number of schooners deepsea-fishing expanded, reaching a high of over 400 on the brink of the First World War. The quantity of fish landed in Gloucester has risen since that time, reaching 350 million pounds in 1970. The increase, however, does not mean that the Gloucester fishermen have prospered.

Clarence Birdseye, who had recognized the potential in quickfreezing food during winters in Nova Scotia, developed a refrigeration technology in the early 1920s that allowed fish caught anywhere to be preserved and brought to port in large quantities. This, coupled with the mechanization of the boats themselves, terminated the schooner-dory saltfish industry. Soon large foreign boats were bringing their enormous frozen catches into Birdseye's and a succession of other processing plants on Gloucester's waterfront. The quantity of fish landed increased, but little of it was brought in by Gloucester boats. Refrigeration and the diesel engine gave the edge to the other maritime nations of the North Atlantic.

The fishermen not only became ghosts but a proletariat dependent upon the fish-processing firms ashore for their meager livelihood.

This, then, is the milieu into which the Italians entered when they came to Gloucester. The first performance of the St. Peter's Fiesta was the year before the last saltfishing schooner left Gloucester harbor.

Italian Americans

The first Italian name in Gloucester chronicles is that of Reverend Luigi Acquarone, who served as parish priest to a congregation of Portuguese and Irish Roman Catholics from 1857 until 1871. He was the only Italian parish priest in the history of St. Anne's parish by its centennial in 1955, and he clearly did not serve a community of his countrymen, of whom there were very few in Gloucester. Perhaps he was chosen because he was familiar with English or with fishing communities; he was not in Gloucester because he was Italian.

There is a great difficulty with the label "Italian," a situation exacerbated by the insensitivity of statisticians and historians. During the 1860s, the modern state of Italy formed out of separate regions. Calabrese, Piemontese, Romans, Neapolitans, and Sicilians were for the first time united under the same government. These "Italians" had (mostly) a common religion and language, but they also had regional folk beliefs and dialects, as well as local traditions of government. The wars and dislocations that terminated in this shaky unity helped encourage emigration to the United States. In 1850, the U.S. census enumerated 3,045 people of Italian origin. Between 1870 and 1914, another four million Italians emigrated from Southern Italy alone, out of a total native population of about fourteen million (De Conde 1971). Though they may have been Sicilians or Calabrese in their native land, in America they were Italians, or "from Italy." Differences that may have meant a great deal to the immigrants, identity itself, were erased by American officials.

The 1895 census of the Commonwealth of Massachusetts indicates that out of a population of 28,211, there were 102 people from Italy in Gloucester. They likely came from Italy by way of Boston, an ironic parallel to the first permanent settlement of Gloucester—religious dissidents from Boston—and they probably were Sicilian fishermen. The register of ships annually published by the *Gloucester Daily Times* shows no signs of Italian ship ownership up to and well past the turn of the century. The voice of Gloucester is silent about Italians or Sicilians except for a few revealing incidents reported in the newspaper. What was reported reveals more about the attitude toward the Italians than about the community that was taking shape on "the Fort."

On 24 June 1905, for instance, an unnamed Italian sailor is reported to have been injured while fishing. Five years later, on 25 June 1910, the Gloucester "licquor squad" arrested a number of Italians for imbibing. On 28 June of that same year, the son of President William Howard Taft, who summered at Cape Ann, struck an "Italian workman" with his auto. The workman recovered. The Italians were in Gloucester, having accidents and drinking. The date clustering of these early notices is significatnt: June 29, the feast day of St. Peter, was later associated with the Italians in another way.

In late July, 1920, twelve-year-old Homer Smith rescued an unnamed Italian child from drowning in the sea off the fort section of the city. The fort is a jutting headland, once occupied by a Revolutionary War bastion. After the fort's demise it became a cluster of tenements and saloons frequented by fishermen. The presence of an Italian child in 1920 marks it as the locus of an Italian settlement. Within fifteen years, the newspaper progressed from suggesting the proclivities of Italian workingmen to allowing for the existence of families and children apparently as clumsy as their parents.

One month later, the *Times* reported another Italian "incident," which suggested that the Italians were established and were moving in a way that disturbed the dominant voice of the city. An Italian fruit dealer (he was not given a name) who had planned to open a store on Washington Street had disappeared and was missing for over a week. The man had sold his old store, stocked the new store, and waited for a licence. The newspaper wryly added that during the week since the man's abrupt departure, the new store had not been opened and its stock "has long since passed the edible stage." The newspaper allowed no space for the man's family's response to this situation; it was not a matter for further inquiry. This was the voice of Gloucester describing what happens to a man with the temerity to move his business out of the Italian section and toward the center of the town. The rotting fruit was the body of the man.

The newspaper speaks of strange foreigners, without personal names, on the fringes of Gloucester society. The "Italians" were actually Sicilians living an independent life in Gloucester. Their voice is faint because they never embodied it self-consciously in newspapers, libraries, or monuments, because the earliest years can be heard only in the words of a few survivors, all of whom disagree with each other.

Italian immigrants came to Gloucester from coastal towns in Sicily-Sciacca, Messina and others—towns with millennia of maritime tradition. Listening to the desendants of these immigrants recount the origins of their community, I was immediately aware of all the divisions covered by the label "Italian" or "Sicilian." Town loyalty and family identity were not obliterated by the move to America. Even after years of appearing unified and of single purpose to the outside world, the Gloucester Italians (I use the word they use) still recall the divisions that increased the difficulty of making a life in America. They were not the "Italians" the Gloucester townspeople thought they were.

The descendants of Captain Sebastian Scola claim that he was the first Italian to settle in the Fort, in 1905. He was not a captain then, but a fisherman working on a trawler. Others disagree, saying that Sicilians came from Boston to Gloucester in 1895, fished out of dories beyond Eastern Point, and took lodgings on the Fort, then an Irish enclave of shacks and bars. The winters there were hard because of the wind that ripped off the bay and swept into the poorly insulated houses. Nor were the Irish very friendly. The taste for popular genealogy, encouraged by the publication of *The Godfather*, probably shaped these reminiscences. Anyone I spoke to about beginnings was full of the same tale of poor immigrants weathering it out and rising to affluence, or at least comfort. Each family had its own story about life on the Fort and disputed priorities with the others. Their voice was a texture of marriages, births, deaths and, if confiding, of family quarrels.

The *Gloucester Daily Times* records the existence of an "Italian bark" in its 1905 ship list, so Captain Scola's legendary settlement on the Fort coincided with an equally significant advance in the community's main livelihood. The word bark, in the nautical parlance of the time, designated a small boat, a fishing smack, smaller than a schooner but of more account than a dory. Again, there is no agreement about priorities in the community. During the 1920s the ships (like the people) cease to be anonymous and the newspaper begins to list schooners with names like St. Peter (not *San Pietro*) and St. Nicholas (not *San Niccolo*). An elderly fisherman recalled that Italians purchased used schooners and trawlers before 1920, but they did not change the original names for fear of harrassment, or because they believed that a lucky boat (one that stayed afloat and caught fish) would lose its luck with tampering.

Fishing was very bad after the First World War and, people recall, many boats were for sale. Discussion of Italians buying boats emphasized the good deals but also the unsafe and unsanitary conditions of the crafts. The boats had to be re-outfitted and blessed by a priest. I heard one story of a disaster that befell a man who took out a boat without making these arrangements. The teller hinted, however, that it was more because he failed to pitch the bottom properly than because he neglected obtaining the blessing.

"We took over," one Gloucester Italian captain said, "when the other people left the boats to work in the plants." The "plants" were of course the refrigerated fish-processing plants Birdseye's technology helped expand on the waterfront. (The accuracy of this statement can be assessed only with considerable research into labor history of the 20s and 30s.) The new plants, highly mechanized, may have employed fewer people than the old salt plants. That gaining control over a few boats could be regarded as a takeover reveals the need to see a drama of community success in these acquisitions. Certainly the Italians were equipped to challenge the competition and gain a living where others found it hard to make a profit fishing.

The rise of an upper class among the Italians was the necessary condition for any control of fishing boats. The immigrants duplicated the stratification of their predecessors on their own terms. There was a class of laborers whom the few who rose to dominance could command. Those Italians who hired labor for their own boats were inclined to favor compatriots—family members and fellow villagers from Sicily. These people were then joined to the captains by bonds of patronage that extended beyond the ships into everyday life. The captain's clients were beholden to him for their passage to America, their American citizenship, their livelihood. This "padrone" system was denounced by the newspapers and condemned by government officials as feudalistic, oppressive, exploitative (see Nelli 1964), but it remains to be seen how much different it was from the system which operated on the old dories.

Critics stressed the foreignness of the padrone system because its efficiency threatened the established economic relations. From the Italian viewpoint the ships simply became better organized; they were a comfortable—if that word is ever appropriate—extension of family life on land. The captain was the father and the crew his obedient sons. He cared about them as no American captain could. Old Italian fishermen look back to voyages on the Italian "family" boats. Although the dangers of deepsea fishing in the days before radar and total mechanization had not been lessened, they speak affectionately of relations on board the ships and cooperation in the common task. Like all sailors today, they sweeten the past to sour the present, for which they have little love.

In acquiring their own boats and filling them with their own society the Italians won the right to a voice sounding much like their predecessors, perhaps in Sicilian dialect, but speaking proudly of the same courage and fortitude that the Yankees were detailing in books. Concentrating upon the Italian fishermen automatically excludes other Italian voices: the women's voice, the voice of the quarrymen who worked in the marble industry, the voice of the shopkeepers. There are quarrels and dissents; there are those who question the importance of fishing. But the Gloucester Italians can speak together as fishermen. They retain that voice through time, and when they announce themselves as Italians and then as Italian Americans, they are fishermen. Their voice is their speech set against the uniformity of the Gloucester speech from which they have been excluded.

The St. Peter's Fiesta is an important public announcement of the fishermen as Italian Americans. Whereas the old Gloucesterites early named their historic houses and built their museums, the Italians, as soon as they could, started to speak in the voice of the fiesta. It encourages two stereotypes and an oversimplified opposition to see the Italians as gay and fun-loving and the Yankees as dour and gray, the Italians as animated and the Yankees as hidebound. The Italians choose to speak in celebrations played against the Yankees' rehearsal of the past in built and written memories. Italians and Yankees celebrate publicly and privately, and neither group is as simple or as simply opposed to the other as misinformation might imply. Stereotypes create ethnic groups rather than the other way around. But the St. Peter's Fiesta arose as the Italians gained a voice in Gloucester and had to sound different from the voice already heard. There are a great many other Italian voices in Gloucester, but for the purposes of this book the fiesta is all the voices together filling the spaces by the sea.

CHAPTER 3

Memories

Memory and celebration are reciprocally evocative. We commemorate the places we come from, the experiences we share, the myths and histories with which our identity is connected. Celebration objectifies memory, rendering it in public form and cultural performance. Celebration also designs memory, shaping its moral, aesthetic, and emotional configurations.

The voices of memory and the sounds of celebration are heard in a variety of dramatic traditions, which together constitute what Warner (1959) would have termed the "symbolic life" of the people of Gloucester. We turn here to some of these traditions and to their prominent role in the St. Peter's Fiesta.

Celebration in Gloucester

One night in October, 1900, the fishing vessel of Captain Joseph Mesquita was run down by a Cunard liner. Only one of the sixteen men aboard drowned. The rest were rescued by a passing boat. Afterwards Captain Mesquita fulfilled a vow to bring a Portuguese custom practised in the Azores to the New World. Accordingly, on Trinity Sunday, 1902, the Portuguese in Gloucester carried a silver crown to Our Lady of Good Voyage Church where Captain Mesquita was crowned "imperator" for a brief reign.

The Gloucester Portuguese community traces this custom back to the reign of Queen Isabella, who each year crowned a commoner, who then reigned for a day and distributed food and gifts. The custom, practised in the Azores for centuries, when adopted in Gloucester, in a sense completed the transfer of customs begun with the building of a Portuguese Catholic church on "Portuguese Hill" in the last decade of the nineteenth century. When the church burned down in 1914, it was replaced the following year by the present Our

Lady of Good Voyage Church, copied from a church on the Azorean island of San Miguel. Around the same time, a wooden statue of Our Lady cradling a schooner was brought from the Azores to adorn the church and the yearly crownings. The crowning has been celebrated each spring since 1902. A procession marches from the church to the house of an "imperator," selected from among the members of the Divino Espiritu Santo Club. The event grew into a series of separate crownings and processions and at one time even included a blessing of the fishing fleet—when there was a Portuguese fleet in Gloucester.

In the public display of the crowning, the Portuguese asserted their presence in Gloucester and entered into Gloucester history, albeit on their own terms, with an old country custom. When I first inquired about the "blessing of the fleet" in Gloucester, the chief librarian told me that the Portuguese community has a beautiful church and an annual crowning ceremony, but she was unsure if they still held a fleet blessing. Whereas the Portuguese are a "good" minority and their festival pretty enough to acknowledge, this is not the case with the Italians. On the 75th anniversary of Our Lady of Good Voyage Church, Reverend Joseph Manton equated the statue of Our Lady in the church with the Fishermen's Monument, suggesting a unity more appropriate to the social condition of Gloucester than the more obvious equation of the monument with the Italian St. Peter.

The Portuguese crownings preceded any Italian community display by many years; they started before there was any recognized Italian settlement in Gloucester. Indeed, the Portuguese celebration made the space of Gloucester available to other demonstrations of community solidarity. The crownings and fleet blessing coincided with the fishing boats' first spring trip to the Grand Banks. In this way, the festival was simultaneously a celebration of a Portuguese fleet and an appeal for a good season's voyage. Once the Italians acquired enough boats, they too wished to have a "fleet" and a festival marking their presence in Gloucester. This, however, was not the only motive for a celebration.

Each year the Freemasons were in the habit of parading on June 24 (or the Sunday nearest) through Gloucester. The organizers were fishing captains, or men whose fortunes depended upon fishing. They chose June 24, St. John's Day, for their annual display of solidarity because an old English belief has it that on that day

St. John the Baptist blesses the waters, making it safe to go fishing. The Gloucester Masonic parade was a fishing elite's show of social and economic dominance. In continuing an English custom in America, as Masons, their voice was clear in their annual parade. Yet, when they marched to celebrate their bicentennial in 1970 the streets were empty.

St. Peter's Fiesta

June 24, Walpurgisnacht, Midsummer's Eve, is a festive time throughout Europe. The Roman Catholic Church situated the feast of St. John the Baptist on that day to curtail the pagan activity during the night but this was, as usual, not entirely successful. St. John's Eve was a time for performing love divination. In Sicily, as in the north, St. John's Day marked the beginning of fishing (Pitre 1881). The Sicilian fishermen who settled in Gloucester saw an important holiday usurped by the people whose hold on the fishing industry they were challenging. In 1970 no one recalled if there was conflict between Italians and Masons on St. John's Day. The Italians saw close at hand a summer-solstice feast day strictly their own and not requiring them to confront the Masons over St. John's.

The feast day of Saints Peter and Paul is celebrated on June 29, though in practice St. Peter is usually remembered alone. In Sicily, St. Peter's Day was a time when family estrangements gave way to fleeting conviviality.

> The women, following an ancient usage, each sweeps out her house alone, and then, together with the others, sweep out the street they inhabit. I say "inhabit" because . . . the women live outside, in the courtyards and alleys. Here they dicker, quarrel, gossip while cleaning; only at night do they return to their houses while the men stay out to sleep under the stars (Pitre 1881:v.21, 323).

Pitre describes the riotous feasting in crowded courtyards and alleyways. People who normally hesitated to "open their mouths" outside their home enjoy the hospitality of relatives and neighbors. St. Peter's Day was a feast of hospitality shared among people normally not hospitable.

St. Peter's Day was a recognized holiday among the immigrant Sicilians living on the Fort before it became a public display. In 1970 there were recollections of lavish food and dancing outside: in the cold climate of Gloucester the Sicilian celebration turned into a festival of summer. The heavy winter had lifted and the doors opened; people toasted the return of warmth and outdoor community. And it was equally a feast of conciliation. On this day village and family divisions gave way to the unity of a common language and a common faith. Early St. Peter's Day in Gloucester had the vitality of people discovering they could dance together under the stars. The *Gloucester Daily Times'* reports of drunkenness and accidents around this time of year were an outsider's superficial reaction to the mysterious, threatening tumult in the Italian community. The American tumult on the Fourth of July one week later was not as unfavorably reported.

St. Peter was a fisherman who became the first Pope. His rise from humble beginnings, his vocation and his Roman Catholic associations were each a Sicilian boast and a challenge to the anti-Catholic Masonic Yankee fishing captains. The voice that spoke intimately on June 29 was rising toward a public vocalization in the proximity of the main Masonic display, St. John's, and the main Gloucester/American display, 3–4 July.

By his own account, Captain Salvatore "Sam" Favazza, a boat owner and a powerful man in the Gloucester Italian community, ordered a full-size statue of St. Peter from Daprato, a sculptor living in Charlestown. Captain Favazza came originally from Terrisini in Sicily, where St. Peter's Feast was celebrated annually. When the statue arrived, Captain Favazza asked Daprato to make it look fifty years old like the Captain himself. Its home became the window in the fishing supplies store run by Peter Favazza in Market Square. The women of the community collected enough money by taxing the boats to build an altar for the statue outside the window. There the statue remained, exhibited outside on St. Peter's Day, inside for the rest of the year, a guardian of the boats departing from the nearby wharves, a presence before the transactions on the square, and a reminder of Captain Favazza's particular act of devotion.

A characteristic element of Sicilian (as indeed Italian) patron saints' festivals is a procession in which a figure or banner representing the saint is carried through the streets along a predetermined route (Pitre 1900:xxxiii). The procession may also include spectacular floats, giant figures, *tableaux vivants* with the figure of the saint in the center. With the arrival of the St. Peter

statue it was possible to evoke this tradition in Gloucester. For
St. Peter's Day in 1929 the women of the community persuaded the
men to carry the statue in procession. And so the first St. Peter's Day
procession took place in Gloucester.

The plans laid for the 1929 procession were not much more
detailed than they had been for past celebrations. It was expected
that each family would celebrate the holiday by itself, and that the
procession would provide a brief chance for concerted worship. On
the morning of 28 June 1929 the men removed the statue from the
window shrine in Peter Favazza's warehouse and mounted it on a
platform shouldered by six prominent men. Surrounded by a group
of others, including some relief carriers, these men carried the statue
around the Fort, picking up a procession as they went along. By the
time they had made a full circuit of the Fort and come to Fort Beach
a large crowd clustered around it. Backyard family festivities had
broken up and dissolved into the moving crowd. The statue was
placed on a pedestal on the beach and the parish priest conducted a
brief blessing ceremony. With this, the procession was formally over.
However, when the men lifted the statue and headed back toward the
shrine, the crowd accompanied them and filled the public space of
Market Square. It did not break up after the statue was back in
place, with many of its members remaining in the square talking and
eating until evening fell. When individual family celebrations
resumed later, they had more of an interfamilial character. The
procession had defined a community of all Italians living on the Fort
to celebrate St. Peter's Day as it always had been celebrated in Sicily,
together out under the stars. The Italian village of the Fort no doubt
already existed, but with the 1929 celebration it gained a public voice
that was the combination of all its voices.

The success of this first public statement inspired a wish to
perpetuate that moment in 1929 when the whole community came
together. Each successive performance was ideally a recreation of
that moment, using the means available at the time. The history of
the St. Peter's Fiesta is therefore a paradoxical progression of
changing content trying to attain the same original shape. The idea
of the original shape changes with the passage of time. This is how
the fiesta draws upon and organizes its separate voices into a single
voice. Or, to avoid personification inappropriate to the concept of
festival voice, this is how the organizers and participants find a

common voice in the fiesta. Over its successive performances since 1929, the fiesta has spoken with a number of different voices, each dominated by and assimilated into the pervasive sound of the attempted whole.

The statue and the inspiration for the celebration came from Captain Favazza, who was still alive in 1970. His was a monumental act of devotion to his patron saint, Peter, and at the same time a perpetuation of the customs of his native village, Terrisini. Importing the statue and having its celebration accepted meant that the Terrisini natives took the upper hand in Gloucester over natives of other Sicilian towns, who had other patrons and other festivals. The celebration was at once unification and domination, and it incorporated both elements from the start. The statue was not a symbol alone, but a person. Captain Favazza's extraordinary longevity made the identification seem ordained.

Each fiesta is a memory of its own origin somehow spoken: the history of the fiesta can be traced only through the voices that rise in people's recollections but are actually part of the whole fiesta. Each fiesta recalled is heard in that dominant tone; each fiesta performed is the recollection of the past voices in an order which gives an impression of the original community retrieved. Listening for the past fiestas is hearing any present fiesta strung out over a series of artificially separate voices which, thus heard, seek union in the present fiesta.

St. Peter's Club

The 1930 fiesta and all subsequent performances have been organized by St. Peter's Club. It is a combined religious association, fishermen's service club, and men's recreation society. From its formation, it has been the main men's club and a body of great influence in the Italian community. It resembles other Italian-American saints' clubs in some respects (Sartorio 1918), but is unusual in the singular hegemony it exercises in the Gloucester Italian community. Whereas even in smaller communities there may be several saints' clubs, each composed of members from a different region, town, or city in Italy, Gloucester men have only the one.

The success of the 1929 fiesta inspired the formation within the club of a St. Peter's Fiesta Committee composed of Captain Favazza and two other prominent men. The committee was to marshal the resources of the community to repeat the success of the first fiesta. Each committee member represented a different large family-village concentration and could activate a number of links to overcome the antagonisms that could make another cooperative celebration difficult. Merely obliging people to participate would not lead to a strong fiesta.

The committee recognized, from their position of leadership, that they must offer a festival plan acceptable to all. The number of different interests which they had to placate is difficult to envision. Yet their procedure became clear as early as 1931, when they ran a celebration that was unlike any of the Sicilian St. Peter's festivals *(feste)* which Pitre describes (1881:321–30; 1900:337–40). Instead, the 1931 event conformed to the pattern of village patron saints' festivals that Pitre abstracted from a survey of many examples (1900:xiii–xv). Thus St. Peter's Fiesta in Gloucester took shape as a generalization from tradition rather than as a continuation of any particular tradition. No particular village was favored; the fiesta was for all Italians. The uniqueness of the event is suggested by the title "fiesta," which has taken hold in recent years. Although Spanish, it is more familiar to English speakers than the Italian "festa" and more idiosyncratic than the English "festival."

In 1931, the fiesta opened on 27 June at 4:30 p.m. in the lavishly decorated and brilliantly illuminated public space of the Fort. Another fiesta tradition was begun with the lighting provided by Emilio Mattarazzo of Boston. The first event was a series of official greeting speeches by politicians and church officials. The speakers lauded Italian contributions to America and treated Italian traditions with religious piety. For the rest of Friday evening, an Italian band played Italian melodies while the crowd promenaded under the lights. Late in the evening a professional *fugista* set off a display of fireworks. Of course, separate family feasts were going on the entire time, but the fiesta was a place where individual celebrations came together. The coalescence of 1929 had been institutionalized, or at least spatialized.

The next day, the fiesta recommenced on the Fort's large beach with more band music, followed by aquatic sports, a "greasy pole" contest and a seine-boat race. The greasy pole is an erect flagpole smeared with lubricant which aspirants have to scale, a tradition of the Sicilian festivals Pitre studied. Since the seine-boat crews were established by family affiliations and since each greasy pole contestant had family backing, these events harnessed competition to make a festive spectacle. The 1931 sports reconciled a few bitterly antagonistic groups to the extent that two sworn enemies, both of whom had supported losing teams, attended the victory celebration together. Immediately after the sports came the procession, this time with the addition of marching bands, clubs, floats, and fireworks set off along the line of march. There were floats portraying St. Peter and other religious figures, each the work of a family. Since prizes were awarded, this was another opportunity for orderly competition among families. The procession made its way to Fort Beach for the blessing and then returned to the public space as it had in 1929. This time, however, the statue was not immediately re-enshrined behind the warehouse window. Instead, it stood at an outdoor altar presiding over the gathering as the band played and people visited the food booths for different Italian dishes.

Sunday began with a Mass in honor of St. Peter at St. Anne's Church. The finals of the sports events took place at night followed by another band concert and finally a grand fireworks display. The festival came to an end with the statue's return to its window shrine with much clamor, regret, and weeping.

Italy

The fugista who set off the fireworks display at the 1931 fiesta had been decorated for his artistry by Mussolini, "the widely admired dictator of Italy" according to the *Gloucester Daily Times*. The newspaper was portraying a common sentiment of the period. Mussolini had been prime minister since 1922 and since that time had given the impression that he had done much to repair the war-ravaged economy and the shoddy image with which the First World War had left his country. But his overseas adventures and his later reliance on Hitler qualified the optimism.

Italy had been a major power during the latter part of the nineteenth century. When a New Orleans mob lynched several Italian immigrants in 1898, the U.S. government had to accede to Italian demands for an apology and an investigation, lest the Italian fleet be sent to bombard American cities (Gambino 1974). Italians in America looked back to this age of strength (and to earlier ones) and enthusiastically promoted Mussolini's *risorgimento*. The St. Peter's

Fiesta originated within, and was in part prompted by, this resurgent nationalism. The recounting of Italian accomplishments, the magnificent procession and the athletic displays all celebrated the new glorious Italy. When the Italian diplomatic attaché in Boston visited Gloucester at fiesta time in 1936, he was greeted with a fascist salute by members of the St. Peter's Club and presided over the official events of the fiesta. The 1936 fiesta spawned an excitement, which was shared with other Italian communities across the country (Diggin 1972). But it should be emphasized that enthusiasm for fascism in America was by no means universal in the Italian community, nor was it confined to Italians.

The fiesta salutes celebrated the national identity that had restored pride to a downtrodden minority and impelled the creation of the fiesta. These displays of solidarity continued in the fiestas of the late 1930s. But the 1940 fiesta, which would have been the first wartime fiesta, was cancelled and all the funds collected were contributed to war relief. The fiesta ceased until after the end of the war, in 1946. During the war the Italian community contributed its share to the effort and suffered the anguish of abrupt severance from the native country. The 1946 fiesta centered around the dedication of a plot of land on the Fort, first intended as an Italian church, as a park in honor of two Gloucester Italian-American servicemen who had been killed in action. The same fiesta ran concurrent with a meeting of the Sons of Italy in America, the officials of which occupied the place of honor held by Italian diplomats before the war. The voice of Italy had changed in the fiesta, and Italians had become Italian-Americans.

Women

Accounts of past fiestas emphasized men; indeed, the dominant voice of the fiesta is a male voice. Yet the women are not silent, despite what many think. Their sounds are heard in Pitre's description of the Sicilian St. Peter's Fiesta. They enshrine and decorate the statue once the men have positioned it. They prepare and serve the food for the family feasts which comprise the private celebration of the fiesta; they construct and maintain the home shrines where St. Peter figures prominently among the other saints; they raise the children who inherit the tradition. The adornment of the main altar and the floats that are part of the procession are the work of the community's women.

St. Peter is the external image of male dominance, and his fiesta is the ritual enactment of that dominance: the controling power of St. Peter's Club and the flirtation with fascism before the war are vocalizations of the male preponderance.

Men maintain symbolic dominance within the home, also. St. Joseph stands at the center of the household altar, the Virgin Mary and the Christ Child forming the Holy Family beside him. St. Joseph's Day, 19 March, is a major feast in the Gloucester Italian community, but it is an internal feast, a time for family visits and large meals. The irony is perhaps too delicious to contemplate but it is true, nonetheless, that it is the women of the community who maintain both saints in their shrines. The preeminent appearance of the male saints depends on the exercise of the women's management skills, and not merely domestic management. The women shape and adorn the male-dominated fiesta, suggesting that the display of male dominance is at their behest. Because the men are often away on their fishing boats, the children are in the hands of their mothers more than usual. The women's shaping and adorning the fiesta corresponds to their shaping and adorning the community's males.

During the war, while St. Peter reposed behind his window, the women organized prayer societies to plead for peace and the return of the men abroad in the armed services. The foremost of these societies was the Madonna della Grazia, headed by the formidable Mamma Vita. Her matriarchal sway was so oppressive that another group, the Madonna del Soccorso Society, was established. Prayer meetings were the main celebration, and the household rather than a public space was the focus of community activity, as it had been before the St. Peter's Fiesta begun. After the men returned and the fiesta was revived, the women were forced back into their former roles.

Unlike most Southern Italian women, Sicilian women did not usually help the men at their work (Cohen 1977:121), but so far there has not been any study of women's work outside the home after immigration and during war. The fish-processing industry may have provided unmarried women with low-wage employment of the sort the textile industry provided in New York City. Yans-McLaughlin summarized the conditions of Italian-American women's labor:

> The depreciation of women's work had important practicality in
> an immigrant community where male unemployment was

extremely high. Italian laborers and dock, railroad and construction workers (fishermen can be included here) found themselves out of work five or six months annually . . . These patterns and immigrant perceptions of women's work provide evidence for continuing patriarchal control among Italian-Americans. The Italian woman's economic contributions made family survival possible, yet she apparently remained a silent partner in the marital economic relationship; Italians did not admit their women worked, even to themselves (1977:107).

The women stay inside, generally. The St. Peter's Fiesta is one of the few opportunities they have to "go out." Of course they are not held captive in their home; they visit other homes, other buildings. The St. Peter's Fiesta is nonetheless a time for the opening of doors—one of the few times when women make a public appearance, go out on boats, display their domestic abilities, pray in the open, and so on. The Madonna, who dwells within the enclosed garden, opens the gates and goes forth: the voice of the women is the complex voice of the Madonna coming out of confinement and the domesticated space which the men supposedly dominate. It issues from the interior, which men have always liked to make into a mystery, the better to minimize and ignore it.

It was the women who first prevailed upon the men to carry the statue in procession. Their voice spoke before the fiesta and it continues even when there is no fiesta. When the fiesta is in danger of failing through lack of funds, the women say they must take it back from the men and reorganize; but, in fact, they never have relinquished it. The contrast between women's power and men's power in the fiesta may also be the fiesta's greatest source of laughter. Women live much longer than men, and remember more.

The Church

The first Italian sound in the history of Gloucester was the name of a priest. The voice was heard at the 1929 fiesta in the form of the parish priest's blessing and later at the Mass held at the 1931 fiesta. But the church did not dominate the early fiestas; its vociferations were segregated. Though St. Peter was the first Pope, his labor as a fisherman was celebrated more strongly than his headship of the Church. In Gloucester, his statue was never enshrined in a church, but in a succession of outdoor altars at fiesta time and when not in procession behind the plate glass window of the warehouse and later in the St. Peter's Club during the rest of the year.

As the fiesta grew in size following the Second World War, the role of the Church grew also. However, its role was always kept apart from the main current of the fiesta and was always limited. In the early 1950s, the Mass offered to St. Peter on Sunday morning became a High Pontifical Mass celebrated with the direct approval of the Pope. Church officials, the bishop and eventually the cardinal (Cushing) took part in the solemnities and marched in the procession. Bishop Greco of Louisiana, the only American bishop fluent in the Sicilian dialect, was invited to give a sermon in that language. But the Mass was moved from St. Anne's Church—there never was a strictly Italian church in Gloucester—to Market Square, where a special altar was constructed. The priests had to carry out their rituals on Italian turf and in the appropriate language.

During the early 1950s, a Blessing of the Fleet was added to the fiesta schedule for Sunday. A church dignitary conducted a ceremony on land, casting Holy Water from an aspergil toward the fishing boats gathered offshore. The officiant, bishop or cardinal, then bestowed individual blessings upon the fishing boats from a boat which travelled the harbor. This blessing rivaled and then replaced the Portuguese fleet blessing associated with the crowning ceremony early in the spring. By the mid-1960s the landside blessing was moved to the esplanade before the Fisherman's Monument, and the majority of the boats crowding offshore were yachts. The church readily joined official Gloucester summoning up memories of the town's historic fishing industry. Some of the town officials standing at the rostrum with the bishop were Italian-American. The Italians had appropriated the town's history and were partly absorbed. The church remained distinct.

Tourists

The guide books of Gloucester appeared just slightly after the local histories. People were going "in and around Cape Ann" by 1885 (Webber 1885). They were wealthy city-dwellers who sought the summer cool of the North Shore and had the leisure to investigate local curiosa. Or they were artists following the lead of Fitz Hugh Lane and other marine painters.

In 1910, participants in the Munsey Auto Tour were "induced to lengthen their stay" in Gloucester. Train tours had also been organized for some years. The appearances of commerce had weathered just enough to offer sights to sensibilities eager for maritime quaintness in contrast with the industrial dullness further inland or down the coast. Hildegarde Hawthorne and her "companion" visited Gloucester in 1915 while on a tour of Old Seaport Towns of New England. She saw the artifacts of the fishing trade and the old buildings up on the hills but she did not see any foreigners. C.B. Hawes saw foreigners:

> There are the little cities from the Old World—the Portuguese, the Greeks, the Finns, and others here and there—men and women with the pulse of Italy, of Sweden, of Russia beating in their wrists. You can catch in their names and in their meeting places, if you wish and have discernment, echoes of every movement of importance in Europe, from the Soviet in the north to the Fascisti in the south (1923:218).

The foreigners are part of the picture the tourist should see; they add flavor to the pleasant spectacle of Gloucester and they offer a chance to sample European political movements without ever leaving the United States. A genuine delight. Of course, the labor agitation rocking Lowell and Lawrence made the foreign communities there somewhat less attractive and probably less safe for the tourist, but the foreigners in Gloucester were fishermen and thus more reliable. James B. Connolly saw the foreigners, themselves, as tourists:

> Gloucester is a far-famed port. It also is a cosmopolitan port. Men of many racial strains have long been coming there. They came in the beginning to have a look at the place they had been hearing so much about. Having had a look they quite often settled down there, and usually became good citizens: an adventurous and virile lot, take them full and by, as men should be who go in for the fishing out of Gloucester (1927:67).

This succinct virile statement makes the fishing industry into a tourist melting pot. The foreigners come and become Gloucester fishermen—and luckily, "usually good citizens."

The cheaper, faster cars and the ever-improving roads, the ever-increasing leisure of ever-greater numbers brought mass tourism to Gloucester after the Second World War. The first tour bus arrived on 21 July 1947. The tourists who came during this new phase were snapshot tourists, day-trippers and beach-users, not the painters or sketchers of the earlier phases. They remain anonymous; they do not publish books or portfolios of photographs like their predecessors. The Gloucester community addresses them in advertisement-laden handbooks and through "attractions." These tourists do not have a voice of their own. There is a voice in Gloucester—and in the fiesta—which tries to speak to them.

Since the East Gloucester Yacht Club was founded in 1895 and as the fishing fleet has risen and then declined, the number of pleasure boats has steadily increased. They impede the acquatic sporting events and cram the harbor during the blessing ceremony. The fiesta voice heard speaking to them is usually telling them over a bull-horn to get out of the way. Their only response is the voice of their sirens used whenever a contest is won. The town of Gloucester and the fiesta have changed to suit the tourists.

PART TWO

CONVERSATIONS

CHAPTER 4

Discontent

Listening to the talk of the men in the bars and at St. Peter's Club during the late spring of 1970 was hearing complaint after complaint. Fishing was poor and prices were bad. Codfish were but a dream. The local office of the Bureau of Fisheries was encouraging the fishermen to catch herring, since the yearly quota on haddock was obviously going to be met early, and shrimp fishing, the usual last resort, was not very profitable. To go after herring, not a groundfish, the men had to modify their boats again just after having modified them for shrimp. "More money down the toilet, and what do I get? Rotten herring I got to sell at their (the fish processing companies') price." The market is usually bad at the beginning of the season, but it had been consistently miserable for years running and was not getting any better as spring turned to summer and sailings were more regular. "The fish they want, I can't catch, and the fish I catch they don't want. How am I gonna get enough to send my kid to college so he don't hafta fish like me?"

On 4 June 1970, the "Johnnie and Nick" sank. It was a 25-year-old codfishing trawler owned by the Parisi family. In recent years it had been converted for shrimp fishing. "It just opened up somewhere and started to go down fast," the captain said repeatedly to the newspaper reporter, who languidly covered the event. The captain and crew were rescued by another Italian boat which came in response to a radio distress call. The captain of the rescue boat suffered an injury in the operation and had to be flown to an onshore hospital by a Coast Guard helicopter.

Then, on 10 June, a Russian boat collided with a Gloucester (Italian) codfishing boat and left a gaping hole in the hull. The Gloucester boat limped back to port. The captain and crew quickly had it placed in conspicuous drydock and spread stories about the rudeness and hostility of the Russians. Their highly efficient factory boats were pulling in all the cod and haddock. U.S. government quotas would not even allow Gloucester fishermen to compete for the fish. And everyone knew that the "Russkies" were spying. "What do they need all that radio equipment for?" And where was the U.S. Coast Guard when it was needed. "They're quick to stop us when we got a little more . . . but they hide from the Russkies." The Norwegians and the English, although not as rough as the Russians, were also taking all the fish. "Why can't they extend the limits?"

The modern fish-processing plants that were spreading over the waterfront also annoyed the fishermen. One plant had monopolized the business and could set the prices paid for the catches. They were not good. When the Gloucester fishermen held out for higher prices, the plant bought fish from the very foreigners who were robbing the Gloucestermen of their catch out on the Banks. As if this were not enough, the management of the plant were conspiring with the town government to edge the Italians out of their living space by knocking down all the old houses and wharves for wider roads and tourist attractions. "Clean up Gloucester, huh, that's what they want. Clean up Gloucester."

A special assisant to the Gloucester town manager addressed a Rotary meeting on 12 June; one of the most respected Italian captains was in the audience and listened to the speech without a sign or motion. The special assistant said that the time had come for Gloucester to leave fishing behind; the fish-processing industry was the only useful remnant of that way of life. The time had come to broaden the tax base by making Gloucester congenial to new industries. The salt marshes encircling the town would be excellent sites for heavy industries. With the revenues from this development the downtown of Gloucester could be renewed and made into a much more attractive place to live and work. No one at the meeting asked any questions.

The Italian captain sat at my table at the Rotary meeting, and the man who had brought me as his guest introduced me to him. One of the members of the St. Peter's Fiesta Committee at the time, he was amused at my project: "You don't have anything better to do in Gloucester?" I was surprised that he had not heard about me from the secretary of St. Peter's Club or from the priest or from other people in the community. "I don't go there much." Nor did the captain live in the Fort area, and he had not been in fishing for a long time. He had a part interest in a few boats and in a fish-processing plant. He told me that the fiesta was one of the few times he went back to the old places. "Nostalgia: I grew up on the Fort . . .I don't go back much. Business." The captain did not want to talk about the fiesta; it was a rotary meeting and there was no time.

At St. Peter's Club, the secretary, Irving Tebo, sat in his office at the front of the club behind the statue's window room. Mr. Tebo was responsible for keeping track of the club's finances, scheduling the use of the facilities, and, as he put it, "keeping the members happy." He was a retired lawyer. From his office, overlooking the floor of the dance hall and bar below, he could see the members of the club drinking, talking, playing cards. When I first went to the club to ask about the fiesta, he found the fiesta committee chairman and introduced me to him on the spot.

The 1970 fiesta program was the same as the 1969 program. In fact, the fiesta committee used the same program sheet and just crossed out 1969. I was told that the fireworks, the procession and the blessing of the fleet all would be same; that all the same people were coming; the town officers, the priest, and the New Orleans bishop to deliver his Sicilian dialect sermon. All of them except . . . (and here he turned over the program booklet and stuck his finger into the photograph of Cardinal Cushing) "all of them except this guy; he's *persona non grata* around here." Mr. Tebo brought out a few past years' fiesta programs. The cardinal decorated the back of each one until 1970's program. Cardinal Cushing had sold St. Peter's High School, which was built during the early 1960s. The Italian community had wanted a Roman Catholic school nearby. After the community considered several other possibilities, the Holy Cross Fathers agreed to serve as teaching and administrative staff. The building was constructed with funds raised from among Italian Catholics of Gloucester and surrounding towns. The prevailing rule required that the building and facilities of any Catholic institution be deeded to the archdiocese of Boston. In 1970, after Cardinal Cushing announced his decision to sell the building, a number of people in the community declared that they would never again trust that rule. Or the cardinal.

The purchaser of the high school was the town of Gloucester. St. Peter's High School was about to become Gloucester High School, no longer a Catholic institution. This sharpened the hurt. The high school was "something for us to be proud of, our own school." Since many Italians had moved out of the Fort and into other parts of town, the Catholic schools were a place where the children would be kept together and exposed to the religion of the community. In Gloucester High School, they would be thrown in with "all sorts of people who aren't Catholics." The sale of the school thus struck at the family life and religion of the community, and required the community to face concrete evidence of its own dissolution.

Not everyone in the Italian community reacted violently to the high school sale. The indifference or mild amusement of some might explain the rage of others. Even a small sample of people revealed a wide range of opinion. "That place cost too much; the town'll keep it up better." "The bastard took away our school." "You know, these people would sell their own kids if they got a good price for them." "So what?" The lack of any concerted community action to prevent the sale, or at least to protest it, was as disturbing as the sale itself.

> We put all our hard work into getting that high school going. What happens? They let it go. Like that. So what, some of them say. It wasn't their money. They didn't take out the loan. No one wants to do anything. Fiesta time is coming. So what? Not much of a fiesta this year.

On 20 June 1970, the *Gloucester Daily Times* published a letter from a St. Peter's Fiesta committeeman that said that the coming fiesta might be the last ever. That is "no joke." Apathy, lack of funds, disregard for the tradition were combining to put an end to the fiesta, "one of the last contacts we have with the enjoyable years of the past," continued the author. The fiesta committee had almost abandoned the 1970 celebration for these very reasons. Surely a fine tradition like the fiesta should not cease, urged the author. The letter ended with a plea to save the fiesta.

The community's disunity was finding expression in the fiesta committee, which had been expressing the different forms of unity since 1930. The voices were coming apart.

CHAPTER **5**

Rehearsal

The 1970 fiesta was celebrated in the same public space that saw the emergence of the first fiesta in 1929. In those days it was a dirt-surfaced open space where the fishermen sold some of the catch they had landed at Town Wharf nearby. "It was only clean around fiesta time," a man volunteered when I was asking about the state of the square during the old fiestas. Today's St. Peter's Square was formerly called Market Square, a name that has persisted among those who hesitate to acknowledge the Italian presence. The square is now an asphalt-covered expanse used most of the year as a parking lot. Its irregular, roughly trapezoidal shape is bordered on two sides by roads and on two others by buildings and the sea.

The Fort

Taking the usual tourist course off Route 128 and into Gloucester, one follows Washington Street (see 8, map 1, below) to the point where it joins Rogers (9) and Commercial Streets (11). The two streets diverge at the inner border of St. Peter's Square (1), a levelling of Gloucester's hilly contours. The seaside edge is defined by the Inner Harbor (2), which was introduced into the land long ago by a series of wharf cuts. Town Landing (3) is at the end of one of these. In 1970 most of the square's sea frontage was covered with buildings, an old warehouse (4) and a new gasoline station (5). A severely warped wooden flooring meets the sea beyond the warehouse. Behind the gas station a cut (6) provides docking for some boats of the Italian fishing fleet. Alongside this dock extends a seafood restaurant, advertising "fish fresh from the boat."

The landside boundary of St. Peter's Square is formed by the spacious intersection of Washington, Rogers and Commercial

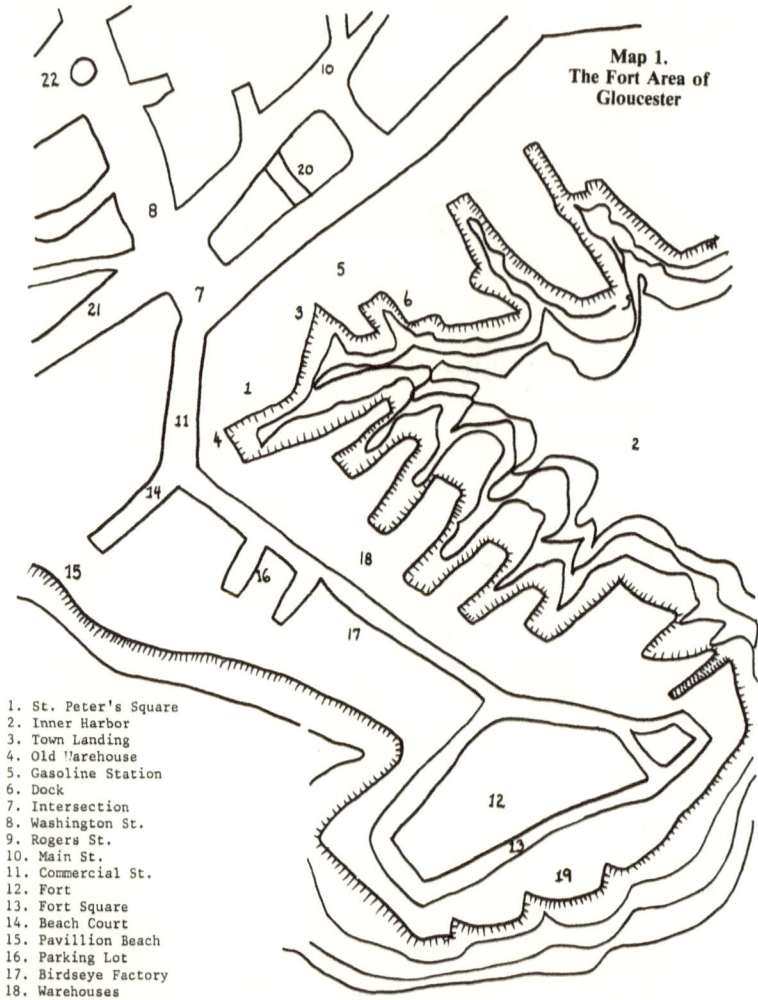

Map 1.
The Fort Area of
Gloucester

1. St. Peter's Square
2. Inner Harbor
3. Town Landing
4. Old Warehouse
5. Gasoline Station
6. Dock
7. Intersection
8. Washington St.
9. Rogers St.
10. Main St.
11. Commercial St.
12. Fort
13. Fort Square
14. Beach Court
15. Pavillion Beach
16. Parking Lot
17. Birdseye Factory
18. Warehouses
19. Fish Packing Plant
20. St. Peter's Club
21. Western Avenue
22. Town Hall Square

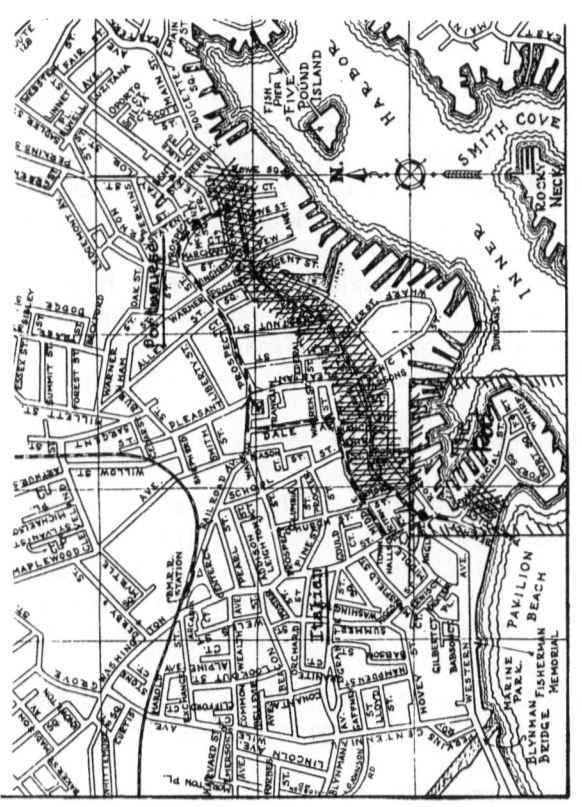

Map 2. Gloucester, Massachusetts

-→-- Route of the Procession
Superimposed square indicates area of Map 1
Cross-hatching ⧗ marks main area of Urban Renewal

Streets (7). Washington Street (8) is a long thoroughfare connecting downtown Gloucester with Route 128. Rogers Street (9), recently widened to accommodate refrigerated trucks and heavy tourist traffic, stretches along Gloucester's seafront, passing Main Street (10) on the other side of the town. Commercial Street (11) runs from the intersection along the narrow peninsula to the Fort (12), where it encircles (or triangulates) Fort Square (13). Stemming off Commercial Street just as it passes St. Peter's Square is Beach Court (14), a dead-end street crowded with tenements housing Italian families. Beyond Beach Court, but accessible through it, lies Pavillion Beach (15), which extends up the shoreline right to the edge of the Fort. Further down Commercial Street are two similar dead-end streets, Pascucci Court and Commercial Court, but they and the structures that stood along them have been wiped out, leaving a rough stony space now used as a parking lot (16). Contiguous to the lot is the "old Birdseye factory" (17), where Clarence Birdseye put his revolutionary fish-saving technique into practice in the 1920s. The opposite side of the street (18) is covered with a ramshackle collection of warehouses, wharves, docks and other waterfront sights. A decrepit fish-packing plant (19) fills the remaining portion of the seaward fringe.

St. Peter's Square used to fringe the original Italian residential area; today, neither the Square nor the new St. Peter's Club (20) is central to the Italian community, with the population spreading along Washington Street and Western Avenue (21) into the large developing sectors beyond Town Hall Square (22). New Italian stores have opened on Washington Street; however, the Fort, the square and the west end of Main Street are still considered the symbolic center of the community.

Returning to the square for the fiesta is returning to the beginnings of the community. But it is also a return to the sea.

Bunting, Lights and Altar

Photographs show the conspicuous display of the Italian flag during the early fiesta celebrations; after World War II the American flag joined the Italian flag in all settings. The statue of St. Peter in the club's window shrine is also flanked by two flags. The flags are removed when the statue is carried in procession, placed on either side of the altar, and returned to the shrine with the statue. All the flags appearing in the fiesta are reflections of this central pair.

As if to turn the entire fiesta space into a flag-flanked shrine, bunting is the first decoration to appear—fan-shaped parade bunting in both Italian and American colors. Workmen begin hanging it from the façades of stores along the west end of Main Street. The St. Peter's Club receives the most effulgent display. According to the secretary of the club, the same firm has handled the decoration since the end of the war. "They still use some of the same bunting, too." The bunting, however, is confined to the Italian-owned buildings on Main Street, mapping the extent of Italian influence.

Merchants who want bunting on their stores are supposed to support the fiesta by contributing to a common fund; or, to put it as bluntly as the club secretary did, "No money, no flags." Several Italian stores sported no bunting. One of them, a deserted front next to St. Peter's Club, obviously had no one to include it in the festive field, but the other stores had no such excuse. Their bare fronts were gaps in the colorful sweep of decoration. The color of the other fronts set them back further into the dull earthen tone of the West End. These stores were people at the fiesta but not in it. Yet their business went on as usual: men shouted and a radio boomed inside the pool hall; the grocer, who was "soon moving uptown," found me an antique can of *cecci cotti* and said rather festively that I could have it for free since no one was likely to buy it now. Old photographs of the West End show it booming with bunting and other florid decorations during fiesta time. The loss was measurable in appearances.

The next step in the preparation was the appropriation of a large portion of the square by two large flat-bed trucks. They were stacked with brightly painted red poles which the same anonymous workmen began to stand in pairs across the street from each other down the length of Commercial Street to the former site of Pascucci Court and up to the junction of Commercial and Rogers Streets (see Map 1). The poles were each about 20 feet high and stood upon cross-shaped bases, which stabilized them on the ground. Once the poles were in place, the workmen began to position wire-frame flower shapes, one end attached to each pole, the open stem curving upward to end in a pair of leaves and a five-petal blossom about halfway across the street. There, it nearly met another rising from the pole on the opposite side of the street to make a broken arch. The stem and leaves were woven with green plastic, the head with light yellow, and the whole shape was lined with lightbulbs hung down from the frame, catching the light of the sun. The flowers formed an arcade down Commercial Street along the periphery of St. Peter's Square.

The workmen were part of a firm specializing in fiestas. Founded by Emilio Mattarazzo some years before, it had for years handled the decorations for many of the Italian festivals held in Boston and surrounding towns. The recent death of the founder left the firm's business in the hands of his sons; that they were continuing their father's work was evident from the firm's style of decoration: the same flowers and the same altar were everywhere in and about Boston one weekend after another during the summer of 1970. Respect for "the old man" kept festival sponsors from complaining, but it did not resolve doubts about the sons' ability to craft festivals as their father had. The death of a man who had long performed so basic a service was too easily symbolic of a greater loss; the sons had a very heavy burden to carry. Even if their decorations were exemplary, they would be criticized because "things are not the same as they were before, when your father was around."

The design of festivals, from the stringing of lights to the setting off of fireworks, is an ancient art in Italy, an art requiring appreciation and criticism. An elderly man who had been going to festivals "for a hundred years" and watching them get worse because they were moving away from the real purpose, to "praise the saint and have a good time," remarked that the lights just "didn't look the way they did before, when the old man was telling them how to put them up." The men around the table at the St. Peter's Club took this as a typical old man's nostalgia for the good old days. But, in fact, the commentator was exercising a right long since forgotten to criticize the decorations. He was complaining that the present generation's failure to evaluate festival setups had made the fiesta worse. He called attention to the fiesta procession on Sunday: "It's nothing but a parade." And he accused the fiesta committee of not putting enough money into the decorations. The ancient celebration disappeared once it no longer played to the ancient audience. Only the trappings remained. "Look, pop, the lights are the same as last year."

The day the workmen were finishing off the erection of the flower arches, an incident occurred on the street below. An outsized refrigerated truck, taking advantage of a gap in the traffic flow, lumbered down Commercial Street toward the fish-packing plant and struck one of the poles, bringing a flower down over its hood. This meant that a lot of bulbs would have to be replaced to restore the design. The driver leapt out, ascertained that there were no injuries, and began to curse the workmen, partly in English and partly in Italian, for obstructing his route. The workmen replied in the same vein and the same mixture of languages that fiesta time was approaching and he could damn well watch himself around the square. Then one workman faced off the driver and the others grabbed tools. A crowd gathered, some vocally backing the irate truck driver with complaints about the nuisance all the poles and wires were creating, some just watching, trying not to get involved. The action turned into a tableau and then dissolved, since there was no way to resolve the dispute. A few knots of conversationalists remained while the workmen, grumbling, turned to the task of assessing the damage to the lightbulbs and the truck driver put his vehicle into motion, screamed a parting curse, received one back and burned rubber (hard to do with a refrigerated truck) heading toward the packing plant. Impressed with the performance, the workmen started laughing among themselves.

The entire fishing fleet was supposed to return for St. Peter's Fiesta and ride at anchor all decked out until the Blessing of the Fleet on fiesta Sunday. The boats were beginning to reappear at Town Landing and along the wharf near the restaurant. It was believed that if a captain did not return in time, St. Peter would wreck his boat. "Or if St. Peter doesn't, his wife will," said Father Buchler, the parish priest at St. Anne's Church. Father Buchler was especially close to the women because he saw them the most. The men attended church only on holidays. The return of the boats brings families together again. The boats are also decked out with streamers in the rigging so that no area of Italian influence will go undecorated. Some of the boats still carry St. Peter shrines near the radio equipment, where help is most likely to be sought during distress at sea. These the women renew as a sign of their rejoicing.

The next component of the fiesta that took shape on St. Peter's Square was the altar-shrine. On the seaward side of the square, back against the blank warehouse, the workmen pieced together a skeleton of wood. The emergence of this form cleared most of the cars away from the square and left an empty space where children rode their bikes. The workmen carefully fastened sheets of red and white paper and pieces of metallic foil to the structure, using a great volume of pins. Before ever deigning to describe the fiesta in any detail, the *Gloucester Daily Times* did report that 500 pounds of pins were used to hold the covering to the frame. The statistic was repeated from year to year in the newspaper and in the fiesta pamphlet, a wonder which everyone could accept. Yet, when I asked one of the workmen how many pounds of pins were used in the altar, he replied, "Pins, we don't use no pins. We got tacks here; good strong tacks. Wind come in from the sea, blow the thing away you got pins. 500 pounds tacks."

The application of the covering completed the façade. A platform extended forward from the lower portion of the altar and stretched all along its length. Steps rose from the ground level up to the main floor of the platform, continuing up the façade, into a deep, curved apse that occupied the center of the façade. At the summit of the steps stood a small platform where the statue would stand during most of the fiesta. The façade arched over this cavity in a pointed peak capped by a cross. Flanking the central apse left and right were three panels in paper and foil, each topped by a diamond-shaped finial. Foil columns separated the panel sections and each side of the wide, flat altar terminated in a broad column. The outline of the altar was strung with lightbulbs not yet illuminated.

The entire aspect of the altar was said to resemble the front of a cathedral in Italy; people even ventured to say which cathedral, the most popular choice being "the cathedral in Messina." But when the same altar appeared in Boston for St. Anthony's or St. Rocco's Feast, it was "the cathedral in Naples" or "the cathedral in Pisa." This all-purpose form sometimes appeared without some or all of its side columns, or without some of the more elaborate finial work. But it was always the same apse for the statue or sacred picture around which the feast (literally) centered. The altar was a roving structural synthesis of all Italian feasts.

The Gloucester construction of the altar was the fullest and most splendid of all altars. The space of St. Peter's Square provided room for the expansion which the close streets of Boston's North End, for instance, seriously restricted. Yet the boxed-in effect of the Boston altars had been the standard in Gloucester up to 1967. Before that time the altar was set up on Commercial Street with its back toward Beach Court, a diadem shining on the crowd of tenements and warehouses of that location. When the residents of Beach Court complained in 1967 that there was too much noise from the band and crowd and that there was enough traffic congestion on their street without the altar blocking the entrance, the altar was moved to St. Peter's Square.

Projecting forward from each side of the altar, three in a row, were tall wire forms wrapped with orange plastic, meant to suggest candles. They also were lined with lightbulbs. Their positioning created a corridor before the altar. With the erection of the candles the altar space was completed—or, more properly, its incompleteness was specified. All centered around the empty apse in the middle of the altar where the statue of St. Peter, still in St. Peter's Club, was destined to reside during fiesta time. Conversely, fiesta time was now defined as the time when the statue was there. A corridor leading through the altar space and up the stairs into the apse was the line along which the statue would travel.

Pieces of a conversation on the eve of the fiesta reveal that the setting had yet to create the spirit that observers associate with celebration:

> "So when's it gonna start."
>
> "Huh?"
>
> "The feast, you know, St. Peter's?"
>
> "I don't know. Maybe tomorrow."
>
> "It starts when they turn on the lights?"
>
> "Maybe. Look, you wanna know, get a paper. They give it all there."
>
> "I thought you'd have some special information."
>
> "Not a chance. Big secret. Go inside St. Peter's Club here. They know (ha, ha)."
>
> (An old man came out of the rear door of St. Peter's club.) "So when they gonna start the altar?"
>
> "Tomorrow. Friday. We take the statue out of the window and put it in that place there (pointing to the altar)."
>
> "This guy didn't know."
>
> "Yeah. He knows. He just don't want to tell."
>
> "I didn't know when the statue goes in, that's what he asked me."
>
> "I didn't ask you that; I asked you when the feast starts. It all

looks ready and the weather says rain tomorrow.''
"Rain or shine, the statue goes in tomorrow.''
"It always rains on fiesta weekend.''
"Yeah. It always rains, and once it snowed.''
"Did it?''
"Yeah. Ask my father. Papa, didn't it snow once during the fiesta?''
"What? Snow? Who told you that?''
"Mrs. Parisi. She said it started coming down just as they were putting the statue in.''
"She wants to tell about that, let her. We get good weather for the fiesta.''
"Sure." (The young man with the newspaper went into St. Peter's Club.)
"Papa, we need to stop for milk.''

To the left of the altar, beyond the boundary formed by the tall candle forms, was the dark snaky collection of carnival rides that had accumulated there as the altar was being assembled on the right side. They filled the space between the candles and the gas station on the far side of the square. It was an itinerant carnival contracted by the fiesta committee to provide the amusements for the fiesta. The side of the long corrugated aluminum truck read "Lawrence Carr Shows" and bragged in curving script that it had been at the Bangor, Maine State Fair in 1968. The rides offered were familiar: a small ferris wheel, electric crazy cars, and the octopus, each with its own tiny ticket booth, dark and uninviting. They were a whole continent of separate experience appended to the fiesta.

In recalling the state of the fiesta I remember mainly the space, because for me the space itself was where the fiesta was played out, though the text I should have been reading was the clash between the orderly space of the altar and the crazy space of the carnival. What was going on inside the Italian community, the private houses, and St. Peter's Club gave way to the seductive dichotomy of the space itself. Not only Turner and Geertz, but the previous generation of anthropologists were with me: Ruth Benedict pointing to the Apollonian altar space next to the Dionysian carnival; Levi-Strauss admiring the symmetry and asymmetry of the one and the other. And, of course, Burke giving me the right to think as a dramatist as long as the materials were present. Try as I may to make it otherwise, I am doomed to take up the enormously suggestive split between carnival and altar, which was the first completed structure of the fiesta. Altar/thesis, carnival/antithesis—and the fiesta itself as synthesis. As in Brecht's epic theater, the plot was deliberately familiar in order to bring greater attention to the drama's dialectical exposition. This fiesta was a good deal like epic theater performed perhaps by a provincial troupe.

I find myself extending the order of the fiesta space throughout the Italian community and willing to believe that it was the intention of the fiesta committee to do exactly this. The order of the public altar is the order of the family altar and the ship's altar challenged by the carnival, which broods on the side. I must devoutly (anthropologically) succumb to this temptation—Turner and Geertz demand that—but never be fully persuaded as they might be that the carnival is all the carnival there is, contained in its symbolic opposition to the altar. A higher carnival there no doubt was, one in which carnival and altar were not opposed or joined together but remained terrifyingly separate, the common ruin of a fractured unity: Bakhtin's great carnival crying to get through and dissipate memory.

A man, unzipping his fly, confided to me that he was going to pee against the altar ("not the holy part"), because that way nothing worse could happen to it. The rehearsal was nearing an end.

CHAPTER **6**

Reconstruction

The social construction of the St. Peter's Fiesta is a symbolic reconstruction of the Gloucester Italian community. Role, obligation, status, and power are the elements of the reconstructive process. The festival repertory offers a variety of patterns in which these elements can be arranged. The organization of crews for carrying the statue of St. Peter exemplifies one such pattern, while the organization of boat-racing crews exemplifies quite another. Taken together, these patterns pronounce their own voice, amplifying the sense of sympolic schism that pervades the community's celebration.

The Weight of Tradition

The statue of Saint Peter is quite a heavy object. Each year fiesta literature proclaims its weight to be over 900 pounds. During the enshrinement and the various processions it is carried about on a platform supported by a long pole on each side. Eight men carry the statue: on each side two hold the front and rear protruding ends of the pole, and another four shoulder the platform front and back. If the weight were evenly distributed, each man would be carrying about 125 pounds. This is not excessive for a short distance, but bearing that burden over the three-mile course of the Sunday procession is hard, even for a young man. A relief crew takes over at a point halfway through the procession, and there are always men accompanying the crew who can replace a flagging bearer. In all, about eighteen make up the statue-carrying group for any fiesta.

Recruitment to the statue-carrying group is motivated by a complex of hope, ambition, and obligation. Carrying the statue is a Christian act of bearing the burden of sins in imitation of Christ struggling beneath the cross. The pain and discomfort of the statue carriers is a vivid expression of the strength of their piety and the purity of their faith. Suffering symbolically in this way belongs to the class of pietistic self-mortifications well known in Italian popular Christianity: walking barefoot, flagellation, long fasting. As the men swelter beneath their load, they chant a drawn, mournful responsorial praising St. Peter while women and children alongside them mop their brows with white cloths, just as the women comforted Christ on his ascent of Mt. Calvary.

Men might take up this Christ-like role with a wish in mind. By way of recompense (notions of how this works vary greatly), a carrier can expect divine intervention. His physical anguish will catch the saint's attention and bring his help to a personal or family problem. Some make a vow: "I carried the statue to make my daughter better; I said that if I carry the statue, St. Peter will heal my daughter," said a captain clearly too old to carry the statue. But he did for a very short distance, long enough, he felt, to bring about an improvement in his ailing daughter's health. A man can "arrange" with the saint to go so far and do so much in return for a set quantity of help. There are hints that men negotiate internally with the saint and that they revise these agreements while carrying the statue. "I asked for good fishing but then part of the way I said I want it better (than good) if I keep up." Sometimes men can be persuaded to carry the statue for another person's vow, for an elderly person who could not stand the burden. In the Boston Italian processions, infirm people have been known to follow the statue group, walking shoeless and carrying candles to indicate that one of the carriers has accepted their vow. I have not seen this in Gloucester, where the delicate stomachs of the tourists seem to have forbidden even mild pietistic demonstrations.

A man might want to bear the statue (or support someone bearing it) in thanks for a favor already received and much appreciated. A normal fishing career sees sufficient rescues to provide the average fisherman with ample reason to want to carry the statue at one time or another. The reason must be pure, however; vows or thanks for the destruction of an enemy or an amorous success are considered illegitimate. "The men who carry the statue wear white clothes because they are clean." They must not sully themselves before picking up the statue, which means no alcohol, nor sex, beforehand.

These enjoinders are designed to assure spiritual purity, but a purity which is immediately equivalent to physical strength.

Besides being a display of religious devotion, the carrying of the statue is an exhibition of power. Men carry the statue to show how strong they are, how strong their family is, how strong the community is. Just to support the weight a man must be strong; to carry it so far he must be stronger. However, strength is not merely physical muscle; it is also moral purity and clarity of purpose. The men who carry the statue are displaying this strength. For young men, the display has an element of bravado. "The girls are watching and the men want to show off. They can show off any time else and no one will look, but if you're underneath a 900 pound statue they have to look. A girl starts thinking about a guy who can do that." Older men may try to carry the statue to prove that they "still can."

If carrying the statue is proof of strength, then stumbling beneath it is proof, not necessarily of weakness but of not knowing the limits of one's own strength. Christ stumbled and fell beneath the weight of the cross, but then he was not supporting part of the weight held by seven other people. A man who hits the ground might trip up the men behind him and cause the statue to tilt or even capsize. Such a disaster is unthinkable. No one could recall it ever happening in Gloucester, though there were a few faint stories about accidents during processions in Boston. (They sounded like the Talmudic stories of unworthy or clumsy men in the party of those bearing the Ark of the Covenant—falling, being struck down, causing cataclysm.) Any man who "goofs off" once in the statue-carrying group is unlikely to be given a second chance. Shouldering the statue represents the strength of the individual, and more than this, it represents the well-being of the entire group.

Strength is readily equated with status in the community, since the statue-carriers are an elite who suffer vicariously for the common good. Certain men or their surrogates inevitably appear in the statue-carrying group. Formerly, the power elite of any Italian community was 'strongly' represented beneath its saint on fiesta day. Men vied with each other for the honor of a place there. Family estrangements and personal rivalries were resolved and caused in the battle for a place. Running counter to this esteem, however, there has always been a contempt for those "suckers" who sweat under the load. This sentiment mixes jealousy with religious cynicism. "If he's so smart why did he do that to himself," a bystander commented while watching a man carrying the statue seek relief from his burden, putting his free hand over his heart. "He's not so great after all."

During the weeks before the fiesta, all these values operate to select those who will carry the statue. The constitution of the statue-carrying group seems self-evident up to the point that it becomes apparent that someone has to carry the statue. Then the competition and the defections begin. In 1970, this decision-making was hampered by the uncertainty of whether the fiesta would take place or not. Once the altar was up and the carnival had appeared, it became apparent that someone had to do the job. It was obvious that Captain Favazza would be the "captain" of the statue carriers as he had been for over forty years. Too old to shoulder the burden himself, he had a strong word in selecting the carriers. Slowly the group formed and then reformed. In fact, the principles of its formation made it always open to change, as someone fell ill, conceived an urgent vow, called in a favor. At the core of the statue-carriers were the stalwarts representing the compromises of village and family rivalries that made the fiesta possible in the first place. But around them the carriers were always in flux, with the possibility of changing during the procession itself. Because the principles of statue-carrying are so deep, however, people in the community tend to think of them as a firm and unchanging group. Whoever they may be, they must symbolize the same things always and thus always seem to be the same people. It was a clear example of how a process imbued with ritual symbolism can transform indeterminancy into constancy (Moore and Myerhoff 1977).

Sport and Social Change

Much more definite was the selection of the seine-boat crews, another major social preliminary of the fiesta. The seine boats compete with each other throughout the fiesta, first in the elimination races on Friday and then in the grand seine-boat race on Saturday afternoon. These boats were once used extensively to lay out the seines but they are not much employed these days because this way of fishing is no longer profitable: the boats are 20-foot-long, propelled by ten oarsmen rowing on both sides from the center. There is a captain and coxswain in each; some also include a child as "mascot."

Seine-boat races are, however, still popular among North Atlantic fishermen. Since the seine-boat teams are already in existence, the fiesta competition is just an opportunity for the Italian crews to display their competence. But seine-boat crews are constituted within the tradition of the fiesta as well. The champions of the previous year return to defend their title; new teams arise specifically to compete in the fiesta contest.

The seine-boat competition is, like the statue-carrying, a display of raw physical prowess and, like the statue-carrying, requires group coordination among men who belong to the same community and pursue the same profession. As seine boats are increasingly peripheral to the main business of the community, and as fewer and fewer of the men involved use seine boats to fish, the competition has acquired the aura of a sport for its own sake. No one has scrupled to revise the fiesta literature to reflect this: the crews must still seem to fishermen to make a game out of a task, even though they are really men playing at a sport.

This sporting orientation dominates the construction of the crews. In previous fiestas (the races have been part of the fiesta since the early 1950s), the crews reflected the rivalries that existed within the fishing fleet and between certain boat-owning families. The captain of each competing crew was also a fishing captain and drew his crew from among the men under his command. He was the patron of the racing crew just as he had been of his fishing crew; he feasted the men and kept watch over them. Their performance was a reflection of his ability to manage their cooperation as he would have done while at sea. In more recent times the captains of the seine-boat crews were just strong personalities who recruited their rowers at large within the community, though family connections were still important in bringing the men together.

The crews, however, ceased to correspond to boat crews and became teams rivaling each other in the race alone. Non-Italian names began to appear in the team lists as captains brought in friends from work or from outside the community. The crews were teams formed to win the race, and they developed careers strictly within the context of the race. A development in 1970 which set the seal on the transition from closed competition to open sport was the introduction of junior seine-boat races for community teenagers. The selection of these crews was predicated entirely upon the assumption that the races are a sport. Only a few of the men involved were fishermen or likely to become fishermen.

I asked a fiesta committee member how they arrange the races. He said, "We don't arrange them; they just happen. That's the part of the fiesta all the people like. The crews show up on the beach when it's time and we have the race. What else you want to know?" (He was, of course, putting me off and telling me to mind my own business. I am, of course, hinting at how close I was to the powerful men of the community.) Yet no amount of inquiry would obtain a schedule of preparations for the races. The committeeman had told me the truth: the races just happen. The community changes, but the idea of order is that there are always crews ready to battle against each other, and there is always a sea for the competition.

I have to rely here on my knowledge that the statue was carried and the boats were raced and my sense that that was the result of precedent and planning. For my knowledge to be any more detailed, I would have to be a community member. I learned enough about the Gloucester Italian community to know that they do not think of the fiesta as details, so that even in having access to the information I would not be in a position to know it as such. There are no participant-observers in/around that community—just different voices.

The statue-carriers and the seine-boat crews were made up of men and involved men in their construction. The women were also at work before the fiesta readying themselves for their role in its celebration. The distinction between men and women in the fiesta is preeminent. The men always appear titled and conspicious (much of the talk of the fiesta is listing men's names), whereas the women make their preparations and participate conspicuously behind the scenes.

Three women's organizations are active in the fiesta, though they are never identified publicly by name. The St. Peter's Club Women's Auxiliary arranges for the decoration of the statue's shrine on the altar, for much of the rest of the procession and for many other anonymous details of the fiesta. The two main prayer societies, the Madonna del Rosario and the Madonna della Grazia, prepare their own exhibits and their own meetings to coincide with the fiesta activities. Their voice rises up into the public sound of the fiesta but it can only be discerned by the deliberate listener. As mentioned previously, the women collectively prepare the backdrop of the fiesta, cooking, cleaning, managing children, and setting the scene for their husbands', fathers' and brothers' performance. Their work is the same as it was before the fiesta existed. The fiesta is a façade given over to men, behind which the women labor. One must know this to attend the fiesta properly. Yet it is hard to know exactly how to attend the women's fiesta. That is a mystery.

PART THREE

POLYLOGUE

CHAPTER 7

Carnival

The voice of Turner (1974) tells us eloquently that symbolic action is dramatically structured. Community festivals lend credibility to his carnivalesque voice. The program of events, often spanning several days, is typically ordered in sequences that parallel the narrative development of a drama, making the occasion as a whole a prolonged version of a stage play. More particularly, the processual form of a *rite de passage* is frequently discernible in festivals (Manning 1983:3–30). Celebrants move through phases that segregate them from their ordinary surroundings, expose them to a reflective depiction of their culture, and then ease their return to quotidian life.

The opening act of the St. Peter's Fiesta, held on the first two days, was dominated by the carnival and an associated assortment of recreational activities meant (with limited success) to generate a festive spirit. The second act, taking place on the third day, was primarily a celebration of the cultural map from which the fiesta drew its repertory of symbols — a map of religious sentiments, ethnic traditions, gender roles, family values, communal identity, and a sense of relationship with the wider society. The final act, held on the fourth day, was a climactic consummation of this celebration, punctuated throughout by a critical and ultimately unresolved disjunction between the fiesta's idealized, residual forms and a number of alternate forms resonant with satirical and subversive significance.

As the fiesta was played out, the volume and variety of its sounds increased. New voices were heard and older ones amplified. We listen now to the polylogue of festive performance.

Expectancy

Thursday, opening day of the fiesta, began with the prospect of sun. A multitiered unit of bleachers was erected projecting from the left side of the altar, its back toward Beach Court and Commercial Street. People in the tenements along Commercial Street posted "No Parking" signs in front of their houses. Men were busy stringing colorful bands of streamers from the masts of boats docked at Town Landing. The hulls of the boats had been freshly repainted green and orange.

Between the carnival and the altar space the food stands were coming alive. Set in a line facing the altar space, the food stands formed a barrier between altar and carnival, and the entrance to the carnival was through two gaps amid the stands. Around noon, several men appeared, rolled up the canvas coverings and put everything in the stands in order, experimentally cooking a few hamburgers on the gas stoves. There were no signs indicating what food was available or the prices charged. I ordered a burger. The man slapped a patty onto the grill, adjusted the gas, and avoiding my eyes asked, "You want the works?" I said yes, and he busied himself unearthing raw onions and tomatoes from a box. He charged me a dollar. Another man behind me asked for pepper steak. The cook started dumping green pepper pieces and onions onto the grill to join the meat dropped there. A hot, spicy smell was in the fiesta air.

The carnival awakened. Ticket lines formed. The heavy shapes of octopus and ferris wheel began to circle. The scratchy music of carnival blared from different speakers everywhere.

As St. Peter's Square grew festive, the seine-boat crews were busy eliminating each other on Fort Beach. Four teams wanted to enter the races, but there was room for only three. A new team, "the Young Scrod," formed of men generally considered too young to take part in the seine-boat races, had issued a challenge. The Young Scrod appeared on the scene late and demanded that they, rather than one of the established teams, row one of the three boats—the *Nina*, the *Pinta*, and the *Santa-Maria*—used in the public competition. They reinforced their challenge by bragging at the bars and the club that they could beat the old men at their own game. There had been a fight. The fiesta committee decided to defuse the confrontation by holding an elimination round. They feared if they did not, there would be trouble during the public competition.

On the beach, the three older teams joked with each other and

Food stand on the periphery of the fiesta space.

with the fiesta committeemen who had come to supervise the happenings. The Young Scrod were intent upon readying their boat for action. They kept quiet but when a cordial challenge circulated among the men of the older crews, that the losers would treat the winners to drinks at the club, the captain of the Young Scrod asked if his crew were included. "No, you kids are too young to drink." And the race was ready.

The boats were supposed to row out from shore at top speed, around some buoys at a set distance, and then return. First, however, they had to line up at equal distances from the shore in the choppy surf. One crew accused another of taking an edge. The ebbing of the tide made any perfectionism laborious. In a lull of the dispute the man in charge gave the signal to go. After some minutes the Young Scrod pulled into shore, followed by the other three teams. A shout announced that the Young Scrod had shorted the buoy. But there had not been a judge's boat accompanying the crews to determine that the rules were kept, and so the Scrod vigorously denied the accusation and claimed victory. In order to avoid a confrontation, the decision was referred to the chairman of the committee.

As the crews trailed back to the square, the captain of the Young Scrod said he was sure that he could persuade one of the older team captains to withdraw; in fact, he knew one of them was eager to pull out of the race. He was right, but the controversy raised by the Young Scrod's challenge enlivened discussion at St. Peter's Club for the rest of the day and night.

A Dance in the Rain

Friday's elements seemed to bedevil the fiesta plan for that day from the first. Heavy rain poured down during the day while violent winds played havoc with the decorations, and an unusual cold forced even the most intrepid fiesta-goers indoors.

When the rain slackened around 5 p.m., the carnival started turning and a few of the food stands were opened. A record-player unit housed in a sound truck was the source of mainly Italian pop favorites: *Santa Lucia, O Sole Mio,* and *That's Amore.* The disc jockey wanted to keep the fiesta spirit going in spite of the rain. A small crowd stood in the altar space eating what they could forage at the few booths. "It always rains at fiesta time." "Yeah it's always like this." As the rain grew heavier, the crowd dissipated. The rides stopped, and the food stands were covered with canvas but remained open. "Even when it's raining like hell people still come here for food. They stick their heads in and say "Gimme a burger.' " The lights still blazed; the loudspeakers still ground out their music onto the empty square.

Inside St. Peter's Club, a fairly large crowd of refugees gathered. A band scheduled to play outdoors had established itself at one end of a large room, and men, women, and children—Italians and outsiders—listened. A few drank; a few danced.

> "It always rains during the fiesta. St. Peter sends us rain so we'll stay inside with the family. He wants us to stay inside and drink the good wine. But the kids, they want to go on the rides. I said to St. Peter, 'stop the rain long enough for the kids to go on the rides and then start it up again.' "

The gathering in the club was unplanned and arbitrary. Yet it was part of the celebration, though the son of a club member was going to be married the following day and he was hosting a private party. No one opposed the intrusion of outsiders. The groom's father wanted the wedding to be part of the fiesta and issued an expansive welcome for everyone to enjoy the feast he had arranged. He was proud to send out for more food "to take care of all these people." Policemen who had been hired to keep order around the fiesta were also invited. The celebration inside or outside had to include "a lot of people having a good time:" the more people and the greater their variety, the more festive the scene. The automatic incorporation of every element into the fiesta space was made a conscious act in this impromptu gathering. "A little rain can't keep the fiesta from going." "Long as we got food, we got the fiesta."

Yet, those inside the club were ever curious about events on the square. "The rain stop yet?" "Who's out there?" Emissaries were sent out to check on conditions and invite people wandering around to come inside and have something to eat. By about 7:30, the rain slackened appreciably and a group left the party, "the people who run the rides." Parents with children followed.

Even though a light drizzle moistened the skin and a fresh salt wind was blowing in from the sea, the rides started up and the food stands opened. If it was at all possible, the fiesta would take place in the square. "This kind of thing don't bother the fishermen. They always have weather like this," declared a man who was not a fisherman. "They like the soup. You want soup now, Eddie?" It was a trifle eerie then. The rides ran on, with only a few children and companionable adults on each. Some danced quietly, moving across the rain-glazed surface of the lot, splashing slightly in the puddles as they went. Men danced together as a sentimental joke. The scene of these couples gliding in the square to a music possibly imaginary reminded me of the scene in Fellini's film "Amarcord," where the young idlers waltz with each other in the fallen leaves outside the abandoned grand ballroom. The silhouettes of people walking across the mist-crowned lights were the ancient inhabitants of festive space, like cave paintings and like a film and then like nothing at all.

A sudden deluge cut the power abruptly. The thin screen of that festive time was yanked away more quickly than a description of the move. There was no sign of movement except for a few shapes closing down the blackened carnival.

Then, a pickup truck roared onto the square. The enshrinement of the statue had been scheduled for that night. Men from the truck and from inside the club converged to haul Saint Peter up the stairs and into the niche in the pouring rain. They shouted to each other as they struggled with the statue. It was impossible to hear what they said through the gnashing of the rain.

CHAPTER **8**

Celebration

Saturday morning dawned sunny. The carnival rides were running early and the food stands were selling pepper steaks for breakfast. The statue of St. Peter lay in its niche, presiding over the altar space and (presumably) the fiesta. Its presence made things different. "You like it?" Mr. Tebo asked when he saw me staring at the figure. His question implied others, "Are you satisfied now? Will you go away and leave us alone?" I fumbled a "Yes, I like it," and then groping to continue the conversation asked, "How did they get it down here?" "They brought it down in a truck," he grunted and walked away. The epiphany, then, had its mechanism.

Women, Men, Flowers, and Transvestites
The altar space was busy with the first major activity, the adornment of the statue and its immediate environs. The women had been enshrining and garlanding statues and finally the St. Peter statue since the community was established. To an outsider it might seem superficial, to the community it was the crux of the fiesta. Or so an outsider trying to think like an insider might tell him/herself. Or so a man doubly an outsider (not a Gloucester Italian and not a woman) might try to read what he sees over the shoulders of the women.

A florist's truck laden with flower bouquets parked in front of the altar and opened its doors. The perfume overwhelmed the square. This seemed to be the signal for a number of women to appear. Formally dressed as though for a ceremony, they joined the delivery man in removing one floral arrangement after another from the back of the truck, all the while consulting labels on the baskets and placing them on the steps of the altar according to a pattern known only to them. Several men from the club stood around watching the women at their task. They did not offer and were not asked to help. When one young man neared the truck with the intent of lifting a basket, the women shooed him off, making the other men laugh. It was a joke. The women place the baskets and the men watch or find something else to do. Only the women know how to deal with flowers.

There were more women handling baskets than there was space on the stairs. They crowded and jostled each other but did not seem to mind the mutual interference as they chatted away. "Did the rain get to St. Peter?" "No, he's alright." "No more rain today and tomorrow." "Your Joey gonna march?" "Put that one closer to the top—look at the board! The bishop's gonna trip over that." Take it away then." "You think we can fit all these?"

As the women talked, an assemblage of flowers grew on the stairs leading up to the statue and on the stairs from the ground up to the altar platform. More flowers lined both sides of the stairways, leaving a narrow aisle up the center. Another truck of flowers arrived. These were large sprays and massive arrangements which dwarfed the modest tulips and daffodils already in place. Gladioli, hollyhocks, roses and lilies abounded. Flowers that never bloomed on Gloucester's hillsides were arrayed on stairs near its harbor. A few more women showed up and together they began to reposition the baskets already set down to show the new displays to advantage.

I watched the flower arranging for a text of social organization. "The women fight a lot when they put down the flowers," one of the men had told me. I expected prestige battles, each woman trying to get her family's or prayer group's basket higher up and closer to the saint. I knew there were women from St. Peter's Club Auxiliary and the two main prayer groups present. They read the tags on the baskets and thus knew who had sent which basket. And they did disagree with each other about the placement of the baskets. A woman stationed one basket right before the saint only to go off and return to find another woman supplanting her selection with another. I listened as best I could to the ensuing words; they always seemed to mask the status tension I believed was at the heart of the adornment. "Doesn't that look better there?" "No, this one is better." "Let's put the one with all the roses, from Parisis, there. The big one blocks St. Peter's feet."

The flower arrangement did not produce the text I was expecting. The women were either agreeing or forgetting they had disagreed about each placement, and the resulting display was visually refined, whether it was socially representational or not. The taller, more ambitious flower pieces went behind the smaller, more numerous baskets. Perhaps the exhibit can be pronounced an image of harmony attained through negotiation, as any harmony is attained in this community. For the sake of appearance the women cleared aside the principle of precedence that dominates the male fiesta and made a place where the aesthetic matters of size, shape, and color could have some force. Right before the axial male figure, there spread a woman's field of flowers collectively beautiful because apportioned and placed without regard to the dominating principle. This was the women's first voice in the fiesta; it always has been.

Down the course of the fiesta the flowers flowed. When baskets disappeared to be replaced by fresh supplements, the flagging flowers showed up rejuvenated in lapels or in the hair of girls: the flowers formed a tidal cascade from the statue. Whoever appeared prominently in the altar space had to be garlanded, enflowered.

A pair of long tables were set up at the foot of the altar stairs and a pair of beach umbrellas erected over chairs behind the tables. On these chairs sat a man and his wife, talking to people who loitered around the table or pulled up chairs to be beside them for talk. The man wore a large square pin, a picture of St. Peter (not of the statue but of the saint himself) surrounded by a black border inscribed with the title "Committeeman" in gold letters across the bottom. A bright red, white and blue fan protruded from the bottom. The picture spanned the area of the pocket to which it was pinned. The woman had an identical pin. It read "Guest."

On the table before the couple was a metal tray holding a quantity of small (about the size of a half-dollar) circular pins with the same St. Peter picture but without the inscription. Beside this tray was a stack of green printed fiesta schedules and souvenir booklets. The booklets were also in green ink and featured a rough photograph of the fleet blessing on the front cover. The inside of the booklet was filled with advertisements and declarations of support along with a list of the 1970 fiesta events. The back cover where the cardinal, the fiesta's ecclesiastical patron should have appeared, was blank.

A ritual ensued, mainly in silence. A person approached the table and showed the Committeeman a bill of any denomination. The Committeeman then handed him or her a straight pin from a container on the table. The contributor took the pin and mounted the stairs to the statue and fixed the bill to one of the green ribbons that hung around the statue's shoulders, the higher the closer to the statue's head. After kneeling before the statue for a minute of silent prayer, the contributor then descended to the front table, received a pin, program, and booklet and joined one of the groups who were standing around and talking.

As St. Peter's emerald green cloth garment became covered with the darker green of the bills, the altar space began to fill with people wearing St. Peter pins and speaking to each other in Italian and in English. In a matter-of-fact tone, they praised the fiesta weather and voiced relief that the fiesta was finally under way. But apart from that, their conversations revolved around family, business, and politics.

At one point, there was an intrusion of transvestite boys. Their arrival was heralded by shouts, whistles, and catcalls from the direction of Commercial Street. They trooped across the altar space—boys between the ages of sixteen and nineteen—dressed not really as women but as boys who had the audacity to put on women's clothing and appear in public. They wore sequined blouses over absurdly overstuffed bras and padded skirts, tight and ill-fitting dance tights. Their faces were marked rather than made up with rouge and lipstick. They waddled and minced and bumped against each other. Wolf whistles filled the air as the people standing around the altar space received them with a mock appreciation their mockery deserved. A man along the route of passage grabbed one of the boys around the waist and received a nasty slap. The troop did not stop to bask in the admiration they inspired, nor did they challenge the main attraction of the altar space any further. They crossed the square and, stopping traffic on Commercial Street, strutted into the rear door of St. Peter's Club, where they were no doubt well received.

> "They're gonna have a lot of fun with those guys in the club. Greasy pole. That's how they dress for the greasy pole. Just for fun. They don't really mean it. Their mothers and sisters and girlfriends give them the clothes and help with the make-up. Every year they come through like that. They look nice, real nice."

The parish priest offered an explanation for the practice of transvestism during the fiesta. "The men of the community are away on boats a lot of the time. The women don't have any other men around so they turn to their young sons and pamper them. They dress them in girls' clothes sometimes." I asked him if he thought the dressing in girls' clothes is (or was) a protection against the evil eye. The *malocchio* is attracted to young males precisely because they are the hope of the family. The death of a male child would hurt the family sorely. The malocchio doesn't bother with girls, who will only be trouble if they live, anyway. The priest said that he had never heard that line of reasoning.

Pitre does not mention transvestism during Sicilian patron saints' fiestas. It is, however, a common feature of celebrations. Informants said that it goes back in Gloucester as far as the fiesta itself. "There was always somebody who put on a skirt and started monkeying around." The greasy pole contest, a Sicilian custom with ancient precedents, provided a focus for clowning and cross-dressing. (It is probably going too far to bring together the erect pole and the women's dress in a sexual reading.)

The outlandish crew is an interruption of the solemnity and congealing family order of the altar space. The interruption is symbolically polyvalent: the boys come as women into the male-focused (St. Peter-centered) space of the altar, yet at the same time mocking the women too by the flamboyance of their dress and manner, with the encouragement of both men and women. The boys are clowns more than transvestites. If their dress and behavior were an inversion of the boys' normal state (and there is evidence it is not), it is even more a combination of male and female in the same people at a time when the two are joined in the altar space. The clowns speak true, just as the flowers near the statue.

The Greasy Pole

No announcement alerted the public to the approach of the time for the games on Pavillion Beach. It was part of the natural rhythm already established to move with the crowd, which had already begun to draw away from the altar space, down Beach Court and onto the beach as five o'clock neared. The threat of more rain limited the size of the crowd, which arranged itself along the narrow beach facing the water. They stood waiting for the greasy pole (pronounced "greezy pole") contest to being.

The setting of the contest was an elevated platform about 200 yards offshore, from which projected a spar 35 feet in length, parallel to and about 50 feet above the surface of the water. At the end of the pole was nailed a red flag on a stick. The water around the platform was crowded with boats. One was delivering a group of contestants, some of them gaudily dressed, to the ladder that led up the platform.

The crowd gathered on the beach was strictly attentive to the contestants as they appeared. Trying to get the attention of individuals, calling them by name and waving, the men, women, and children formed a coterie, hardly a random gathering of spectators. The contest was a community affair.

A sharp, blurting male voice sounded above the calls of the crowd. It was the loudspeaker voice heard in the square. Sporting many different tones and occasions, it tried to be, but never was, the sole voice of the fiesta. Its loudness and command inspired the other voices to make themselves heard. Nevertheless, it announced the greasy pole contest as soon as the rest of the contestants had been ferried out to the platform. "For those who are not familiar with the greasy pole," it began, immediately affirming its authority to explain the rules and object of the contest. The contestants, "young men, sons of Italian fishermen" gather on the offshore platform. Each in turn tries to run the length of the pole and dislodge the flag at the end. The pole is covered with grease "to make it a little harder." The winning contestant receives a savings bond worth $25. There is another competiton Sunday. A bond and a trophy are awarded to the winner of that contest. This trophy, and another for the seine-boat winners, are named after Gloucester Italian servicemen who fell in Vietnam.

Having given this explanation, the voice began to take stock of the space. It asked a boat to return to the beach to ferry more contestants out to the platform, then it asked the contestants remaining on the beach to raise their hands. Boats that had drifted across the line of sight between beach and platform were admonished by the speaker to move clear. Satisfied with the arrangement achieved and mentioning that rain was beginning to fall, the speaker decreed that the contest begin.

The greasy pole contest was comprised of three elements: the activities of the boys out on the platform, the activities of the crowd on the beach and on the boats, and the commentary of the loudspeaker. They were never one consistent manifestation, although the loudspeaker promoted the illusion that this was one single element in the festive whole and was going ahead as planned.

It was the loudspeaker's job—actually its prerogative—to name the contestants as each made his attempt to cross the greasy pole. The naming meant that an order had been established. There were two lists, one at the loudspeaker and one on the platform: the boys came forth in a procession according to the fixed order of these lists. A number of the names included nicknames—"Irish," "Greasy," "Sticky Fingers"—uttered between first and last name. These nicknames were also written down and read. The loudspeaker exercised an editing function: it paused ever so briefly between the two halves of one contestant's name and, completing it without the nickname, said "Sorry, I can't call you by your nickname, Joe."

The speaker referred to the greasy pole history of each boy named. "Last year's champ" or "twice champion" were mentioned several times during the contest. The speaker monitored the appearance and included personal details about the entrants. A singularly ostentatious drag outfit elicited the remark, "He's cute." When the wearer came close to the end of the pole the speaker recalled that he had nearly fallen onto a boat the previous year. "The baker is next," it said before another name; "local football hero," after another. A name clearly not Italian caused it to say "good Italian name."

The performance of each boy did not receive as much comment as the personal description and background. The loudspeaker did not egg on the contestants or try to evaluate their form. It did, however, make a revealing remark after one attempt. The boy was trying to walk out along the pole toward the flag. "They tell me that way doesn't work," said the speaker. The walker fell of the pole halfway.

"Is that Sleepy Pallazolla out there . . . Sleepy Pallazolla. That's an old-timer out there. He's all of thirty-three. Good luck, Sleepy . . . Good luck to your wife and kids, too."

The speaker called out to the boys on the platform once to reestablish the order when one contestant passed up his turn. It announced that one of the contestants had hurt his back but was not seriously injured. If the announced name was incorrect, the contestant waved or the speaker recognized by sight that it was not the person and audibly corrected itself.

Meanwhile, the contestants on the platform seemed to be

conducting their own contest. They fell out of order, followed each other in succession too fast for the speaker to define, or hesitated to send one of their number out. As the contest wore on (it lasted about thirty minutes), their behavior changed. At the beginning, each walker had tried to make a grand rush to capture the flag for himself. But during the second round, when contestants started withdrawing, the remainder did not attempt to reach the flag but sought to shake the pole so fiercely that the flag would come loose of its own accord. This required a more collective effort. It did matter to the contestants who won. But each walker was willing to contribute to the next one's possible victory with the hope that he would not have to walk again. This is the point at which the group demonstrations began. The flag finally fell off when one walker shook the pole violently as he fell near the end. The crowd on the platform jumped in jubilation.

The audience on shore and in the boats screamed, blasted horns, and even let off a few firecrackers when the flag fell. They had been keeping close tabs on the walkers. Each near miss brought a collective gasp from the multitude. People who did not seem to be watching joined the sound. The crowd was doing much besides watching the attempts of the walkers. They were eating, talking to each other, playing in the sand, pursuing petty antagonisms. Several walkers had brought claques who cheered when their name was first mentioned and applauded the attempt no matter how pale. The final wave of expression was so overwhelming that it seemed a mass of sound waiting to be released. The sustained "oohs" were rehearsals. The crowd had finally found its collective fiesta voice, submerging the official voice of the loudspeaker for a moment.

As the crowd fell back to its normal noise level, the loudspeaker moved to the next event, the seine-boat race. Only the wash of the ocean continued unyieldingly.

The Seine-Boat Race

For this event to occur the path of the seine-boats, out to the buoy and back, had to be completely clear. The greasy pole contest had been continually interrupted by boats moving across the field of vision. Now the encroaching boats were an even greater threat because they blocked the seine-boats' passage outland and thus threatened the conduct of the event. The speaker commanded, then urged, then coaxed them to clear the harbor.

The people on the boats were part of the audience, and like all audience members they wanted the best vantagepoint. The view over the water differs from the view from the land. The audience at sea sees it in linear perspective, whereas the shore-based audience watches the whole panorama, seeing the boats in a heat with each other and not caring about lines over the course. Both audiences try to get close to the action: the land audience crowds the shoreline; the sea audience moves as close to the boats as possible. The sea audience impedes the view of the land audience and finally the conduct of the race. Thus the seine-boat race is a match between two audiences and three teams. The two audiences and the three teams fight within and among themselves.

The loudspeaker continued monotonously to coax the boats out of the harbor. It addressed the seine-boat teams, warning them that Sammy Militella, the judge of the contest, would follow in a motor-driven launch and would disqualify anyone breaking the rules. Taking an advantage at the start, or shorting the buoy would bring Sammy's stern rebuke. The loudspeaker announced the names of the teams: the Last Chance, the Young Scrod, and the Gondoliers. The Underdogs had been persuaded to drop out of the contest. There are three seine-boats that race—the Nina, the Pinta, and the Santa Maria—named after the ships of the "famous Italian navigator, Christopher Columbus." The loudspeaker called out the names of the men on each team.

The boats were at the water's edge ready to leave. The surf was choppy and made it hard to line up the boats to the satisfaction of all the men. Just when they seemed ready to start, a boat would pull up ahead, and ensuing screams would delay the judge's call. The crowd by the beach grew bored with its own excitement. The loudspeaker kept on repeating that the boats were ready to start, interspersed with calls for contributions and messages about lost children. A group of children on the beach began to chant "Stevie's gonna lose, Stevie's gonna lose." Stevie was captain of the Young Scrod, in the Pinta. The kids kept up the chorus for a long time. The men riding in the seine-boats shouted at each other and at the judge, who regulated the go-ahead with extreme care. When he finally did gave the signal to take off, the crew of the Santa Maria were so occupied with lining up that they failed to start right away. With no time to protest, they took to the oars.

The contest lasted about seven minutes. As the boats made their way out to the buoy, the loudspeaker tried to maintain a horserace-style description but gave up because it was impossible to tell which boat was in the lead. In addition, a young boy lay injured at the water's edge after coming to blows with another for a better view. The loudspeaker began to appeal for a doctor. During these few minutes, the landside crowd was suspended. With no news about the progress of the race, rumors passed through the crowd that the Pinta was in front. One boat neared the beach ahead of the others. The children's chorus cried, "Go, Pinta, go," their loyalties changing with the tide of the moment, or perhaps just to have the breath of victory. The inevitability of the Pinta's victory was signalled by the squalls of fog horns offshore. The loudspeaker shouted to the people by the beach to clear back since the boats were coming in fast. The Young Scrod in the Pinta hit land to a culminating roar from the crowd. A committee member rushed forward once the boat stopped and handed an American flag on staff to the captain. The Last Chance in the Nina arrived about 30 seconds later and received the Italian flag. The Santa Maria came in a full minute later.

The explosion announcing the boat's arrival lasted while the crew disembarked. Forming behind the flag-bearing captain, they headed away from the beach and down Beach Court. The event was suddenly over. The crowd streamed after the victors, leaving the loudspeaker to talk to itself. The winning team lead the way down Commercial Street to St. Peter's Club. Most of the crowd dissipated into the fiesta space and into parked cars along the way. It was raining lightly.

Inside the club, the first team to arrive had sparked celebrations. The second to arrive modified the tenor by accusing the first of cheating. The resulting shouts and blasphemies became new voices of the fiesta. I asked a committeeman whether the boats coming to shore meant that Columbus had discovered America again. The Committeeman said, "What? No. One time, that's enough."

Voices from the Altar

While the fiesta was away at the beach, St. Peter on the altar had received a shaggy coat of bills. The rides were still running and the food stands still serving supper. In a surprisingly short time the sound truck returned from the beach to the fiesta space and parked alongside the altar. That its voice was in place was clear when it announced to the unassembled multitude that pins and programs were still available in front of the altar. It reminded everyone that the official opening of the fiesta was to take place at the altar at 7 o'clock that evening. The voice dropped away and the Italian popular music of the previous evening poured forth once again. The wind was swift and warm. Rain threatened.

I stopped to talk with an informant, who explained his own celebratory style:

> "You (were) out there on the beach for the sports? I don't go there. It's the same thing every year. They go there, fight it out, then they come back and drink. That makes them fight again. I like to stay around the fiesta. My kids are here somewhere. I give them some money for the rides, tell them to go have a hot dog. That's what I like. A lot of them go out on the boats. Not the fishing boats. They have the sailboats now. You should watch tomorrow at the Blessing. All the sailboats. They used to have it here on the square. Town Landing they call it. Now it's over on Stacey near the captain statue. I don't go. I stay right here as long as the feast goes on. I stay here. No running around."

By 7 p.m. rain was more than a threat. A light drizzle fell on the band members as they filed onto the altar platform and took their places on the chairs set up for them. The band began to play slow dance music. Not entirely Italian, the music included the band's entire repertoire, polkas, marches, waltzes, the occasional band orchestration of a rock song, and wedding music. The band was waiting out the rain, keeping a live presence in the altar space, keeping a fiesta tradition going.

The sound of the band in the altar drew a crowd, mostly teenagers, and tempted them to try dancing, fantastically and in obedience to an old festive urge. A number of children ran through the altar space, making enough noise to drown out the band and confound the dancers, but the dancers were in their own way defiant and evaded the interference as they did the rain. Various kinds of expression were making fiesta in the altar space: the band, the dancers, the children.

At about 8:15, a group of men filed out of the club and a few others arrived in cars, which they parked along Commercial Street. All of them ascended the altar steps. One of the men tested the microphone and announced that they could not wait any longer for the rain to stop, that they would open the fiesta, but that the fireworks scheduled that night would be postponed until Sunday night, when better weather was expected. From the crowd that had formed in the altar space, came an experimental cheer. "I'd like to introduce Monsignor Daniel Sullivan, who is gonna open the St. Peter's Fiesta—with the rain."

Monsignor Sullivan welcomed everyone to the fiesta, referring to it as a "venerable institution." He gave a solemn promise that the weather would be clear in time for the Solemn Pontifical High Mass at 10:45 Sunday morning. His "Buona festa e buona fortuna" received faint applause. Next, the loudspeaker introduced Bishop Greco "who has been coming to the fiesta for some years." The bishop evoked the hope for a rainless Sunday. The loudspeaker apologized parenthetically that the speeches would be short because of the rain, which was on everyone's mind and shoulders. The mayor was introduced and simply addressed the bishops, the committee, and audience, wishing everyone a good fiesta. He retired to perfunctory clapping and a few sonorous boos. The loudspeaker then presented the city council members. After three names and no particular response from the audience, it came to "our City Councilman, Gaspar LaPrada," who received a striking round of applause. The city manager and his silence came next. "Where's our city clerk James Carroll? He's the one that marries everyone around here." There was applause at the mention of marriage. "He's in the audience. You wanna get married, you find 'im in the audience."

A Health Department official "you all know" was next introduced and applauded. Then the loudspeaker named the St. Peter's Fiesta Committee: "Benny Cucurru, the charter member since 1934; Salvatore Favazza (loud applause), is at the present time convalescing from an operation and can't be with us tonight; Jimmy Cairo's right here (wild applause); Salvatore Linquata; Peter Razzi, Junior (some applause); Joseph Linquata; Sam Militella (firm applause), also the president of St. Peter's Club; Nick Delello—is he here?" (applause).

"It now gives me great pleasure to introduce our consul general from Italy, Conci Ottelio." The consul general addressed the assembly in Italian, not in Sicilian dialect, though he singled out "tutti originali di Sicilia" (all natives of Sicily) in the audience. He brought greetings from the people of Italy and wished everyone a good *festa*, concluding with "viva San Pietro."

Monsignor Sullivan introduced the clergy, "most of whom are standing in the crowd with the rest of the people." "Irving Tebo is our secretary of St. Peter's Club and also of the fiesta committee." Mr. Tebo accepted his applause. The rain was growing heavier. "It gives me great pleasure to introduce our representative, Dave Harrison. It took Dave Harrison a long time to find a girl, but when he did he found the prettiest and the best." (cheers)

Harrison spoke briefly:

> "I'm happy to be here tonight. I hope I'll be back again next year. Congressman Michael Harrington was here earlier but he had to leave. I think he was the only smart one here. So I will say that he wanted to be remembered to you people here. Thank you very much."

The attorney general, David Flynn, was introduced and addressed all the politicians and clergy present. He remarked that the weather was more like St. Patrick's Day in Boston than like St. Peter's Fiesta. He apologized for the absence of the governor, "who is busy at the Republican Convention."

> "You know, these (pause) fiestas are like family birthday parties, except this is a birthday party for the city of Gloucester. I am honored that you have invited me to share this festivity and this spirit with you, because as long as this spirit continues in communities like Gloucester and other areas of Massachusetts then we will continue to have a healthy and a vibrant society. Many years of success and a happy and sunny fiesta to all of you in St. Peter (fairly enthusiastic applause). Thank you very, very much."

Leo, the loudspeaker, repeated the announcement that the fireworks were postponed until the following night. "This is the end of the speeches. We had to make it short because of the rain." The clergy, politicians, St. Peter's officials, and ersatz dignitaries filed off the altar-bandstand as the rain fell and the band struck up "The Beer-Barrel Polka." A few impromptu firecrackers were let off, and the band played a while longer. The rain had become part of the fiesta atmosphere, an excuse for licence in the altar space. But the crowd was dispersing and the rain was left to play upon the lights in the emptying spaces.

I asked Mr. Tebo why the fiesta is called a fiesta. He said that it had been going on for years. He guessed it was because "festival" sounded too stuffy—"like the way you guys always talk." "Fiesta" is more like "festa, the Italian word. It means have a good time. Okay, go have one."

Meditation

With a recess in the public fiesta the private festivities continued all over the town, in the club, in the houses, in places hinted but unknown. Much of this was normal weekend festivity given a chambered intensity by the prohibiting rain. The fiesta had been opened and there was no stopping it.

The official opening was a gathering, uprising and intermixture of voices in the altar space. Some voices came simply from spokespersons. The clergy gave blessings and anticipated the Mass of the following morning. The politicians treated the fiesta as an activity of the City of Gloucester and tried to place it in the context of the Commonwealth of Massachusetts. Had a politician of national eminence been present, he probably would have evoked the Americanness of the celebration. The Italian consul spoke with the voice and language of Italy.

Other voices simply made themselves heard through the aggregate. The Italian community was in each utterance of the club officials and in many responses of the crowd. The repeated references to, and the acclamation of, marriage called up family order. No women spoke, and the only reference to women was as wives. The omission was as significant as the equally subtle references to Irish ethnic identity, which seemed juxtaposed to Italian identity as the absence of women was juxtaposed to the presence of men.

Attorney General Flynn's "family birthday party" analogy was perfectly appropriate to the sentiments voiced at the opening. The fiesta is part of the family order that makes for vibrant and healthy communities all over the state, and so belongs to the same category as weddings and birthdays. It brings together the same decent, orderly lot of people in each community. The attorney general made no allusion to Italians; instead, it was Gloucester that was another happy family, having its noisy party. He did not rush through his statement. The attorney general, after all a voice of the established order, expressed the desirability of sweet, compact, family-nice bourgeois festivals all over the state, for which the crowd accorded him a suppressed carnival accolade for suppressed carnival reasons. The mere presence of the mayor was opportunity enough for shaking officialdom with boos. And so the official presence permitted what carnival came through. The firmest articulation of official philosophy, the attorney general's speech, was the carnival's strongest upsurge. No one knew that carnival ignores openings and permissions; it does not have to take advantage of them. The carnival erupted uncertainly and for a moment in the face of its suppression, then calmly receded.

Politicians and ecclesiasts regretted the rain and commanded the sun to appear. They chorused the picture of the bright sun, which, we like to think, always shines at the festival sky. Their speeches and their music (it clearly was their music) were a bullwark against the rain. The fiesta was open; it had one more day to go. All the voices of the fiesta had been heard.

The voice of the fishermen was, however, surprisingly subdued. And it was clear at the official opening that one old fundamental voice, Sam Favazza's, would not be heard from the man himself at the time when all voices had to be personified.

CHAPTER **9**

Consummation

Sunday, as predicted, the sun shone bright and the air was temperate. The altar space was rearranged to accommodate the crowd expected for the Solemn Pontifical High Mass at 10:45 a.m. In the open space before the altar, row after row of folding chairs were set up, and on the altar itself, a long table to hold the ritual apparatus of the Mass. A cross had already been stationed there. A priest in vestments, assisted by altar boys, positioned the remaining implements. The carnival next door was quiet. Nothing could interfere with the decisive utterance of the Church.

Since the Mass was the first major fiesta activity not tampered with by the weather, it acquired an even greater significance. Its celebration was an assertion of an Italian and Catholic presence to be carried forward in the procession immediately afterward.

Rite and Anti-Rite

The Mass, I am sure, is multi-voiced but in the same way that a fossil conglomerate contains different kinds of shells and skeletal matter and speaks in unison only to the careful, educated listener. I can assume that many different listeners were present on Sunday morning, 28 June 1970, in St. Peter's Square in Gloucester, but I doubt that their experience was very important to the fiesta. The Mass simply demanded the space for its voice but that does not necessarily mean that anyone heard it. What people did, what voices were heard while the Mass was being celebrated, was the fiesta.

Dressed in their Sunday best, people began to arrive early, in family groups. In the scramble for chairs, parents made an effort to keep children, sometimes ranging over two generations, next to them, but the children wanted the carnival; they wanted each other.

At first there was reverent silence. But as the crowd grew and the

98

region of folding chairs was populated or claimed by the deposit of coats or baggage or hostile guards, and as the bleachers, very much the second choice, also filled, the tension of the crowd grew plainer. The sun in the cloudless festival sky beat down indiscriminately upon those well positioned at the front and upon those drooping at the back of the bleachers.

A burst of electronic organ music over the loudspeaker and the sounds of the choir, which had assembled on the altar, signaled that the Mass was about to begin. Monsignor Sullivan of the local parish introduced himself, and announced that Bishop Greco of Louisiana, who had been a guest at the fiesta since the early 1950s, would deliver his sermon in the Sicilian dialect as he always had. Bishop Greco would also, for the first time, officiate in the offering of the Mass, replacing Cardinal Cushing, who had sent his regrets that illness prevented him from celebrating the Mass, as he had done at previous fiestas. Bishop Greco declared his pleasure in once again delivering the sermon and, joined by the other officiants, proceeded to begin the Mass.

To an observer, the progress of the Mass could be traced by the initial piety and then growing restiveness of the crowd. They had all attended many Masses, but this was a special Mass—held not only outside, but on the site where the community's fundamental celebration had been held for the last forty years. The priests were elevated and at a distance, as in church. They were occupied with the minutiae of ritual, which some people acknowledged with responses. The sacred music of the choir came off the altar in the sunshine, where, yesterday, the band had played in the rain. Assuming that close attention and firm posture constituted the ideal behavior, the Mass inspired neither. Perhaps the fact that it did not inspire most of the people present threw into relief the concentration of the few who were attentive and inspired.

The formal conditions, Roman Catholic ritual on Italian community ground before St. Peter's statue, were right for a community manifestation. But the crowd's disquiet was the community's disquiet. For the Mass happening there at that time was a manifestation of a collectively which no longer existed before these symbols and in this place. What the community had been in the past is hard to tell. Perhaps it always had been this way. In 1970, the failure of the Mass as a collective experience reflected the state of the Italian community.

Bishop Greco reached the point in the Mass when he went to the microphone to deliver his sermon. At the first syllables of Sicilian dialect the crowd stirred. This was a new and welcome voice. Those who understood listened gratefully; those who did not, and again they were the majority, listened as they listened to the Latin of the Mass—distantly, reverently, and then not at all. Bishop Greco's sermon was on the life of St. Peter. The saint was an example of the faithful husband who had withstood all the trials of his vocation and endured martyrdom to lay the foundation of the Church. He was a simple fisherman who toiled to feed his family . . .

In the Sicilian dialect, with its broad vowels and Arabisms, the bishop eloquently called up the key image of the fiesta, the communion of the Church, the family, the vocation of fishing. As he spoke, his audience decomposed. Children had escaped from their parents and formed an aura of faintly suppressed noise around the island of chairs. Some adults turned to their neighbors to ask what the bishop was saying. Conversations started up. Chairs scraped on the ground.

It would be pleasant to report that the Italian community of the old Fort was reborn there during the bishop's sermon. Perhaps it was. The sermon was permission to be Sicilian. Yet, because it was long, it provided no release from the rigors of the Mass, but rather introduced a greater rigor for those who did not understand the language well enough and who could not turn their incomprehension into a virtue by using it as an excuse to socialize. Locked in the altar space by a wish to keep tradition, these people looked for a way out. They loudly disciplined their children and tried to keep them sitting in the same place; after the children defected, they focused on the squirming teenagers who longed to commence their own vernacular sort of visiting. The fiesta space was islanded with sincere listeners and impatient others.

It is as if the carnival spirit knew about this restlessness and took advantage of it. Part way through the bishop's sermon, the ferris wheel started up. Its coarse squeaking surged against the bishop's inflections. A committee member sprung up from the front row of chairs and ran to the square, where he had a brief yelling match with the ride's operator, who complained that there were a lot of kids waiting to take the ride. Couldn't he run it if he kept it quiet? No, absolutely not. Responding to the force of the denial, the man

The altar and the enshrined statue.

stopped the wheel and coaxed away the children who had already mounted it. Meanwhile the food stands were selling a steady supply of pepper steak and hamburgers to refugees from the sermon. Closing the stands would have been more difficult than shutting down the ferris wheel, since people needed drinks and food to tide themselves over until the Mass ended—those, that is, who were not fasting for Communion. It had been after 11:00 when the sermon started and it was nearing 12:00.

The strain flexed the boundaries of the altar crowd. It developed a fringe of defectors who wanted to leave the altar space but who did not want to go out of earshot of the sermon. And so they lingered near the stands talking to each other. They formed little groups that were simultaneously a refuge for the sermon-bored and a barrier between the altar and the interrupted, resentful carnival. In the few minutes it took them to form, these little conversation groups became a real presence within the fiesta space. They were a quiet, and then not so quiet, human carnival replacing the mechanical carnival shut down by the solemnity of the Mass.

When the sermon finally ended, the Mass proceeded into its most solemn parts—the Offertory, the Consecration, and the Communion. By this time, however, the altar space had shrunk. On the new periphery people stood, as they had during the sermon, and talked and ate and enjoyed what was festive about these activities. They were not defying the Church. They were in a place apart from the Mass which no longer concerned them. Those in the redefined altar space were strict in their observance.

Another 40 minutes elapsed before the bishop gave the final benediction: Ite Missa est (Go, the Mass is ended). The carnival rides started up as if a restraining hand had been removed from them. People poured out of the altar space in all directions. It was time to carry the statue of St. Peter through the streets.

Procession

The procession was designed to emerge from the altar space after the Mass, go round the city of Gloucester by a predetermined route (see Map 2), and return to the altar space in time for the Blessing of the Fleet from Town Landing and the final games on Pavillion Beach. The day's events were to be one concatenated series from Mass to sports. The ideal fiesta-goer passed from sacred to profane and from land to sea following the course of the fiesta timetable.

A procession can be watched in several different ways. The fixed observer can stand at one point and watch the procession pass phase by phase: he or she can follow the procession; he or she can suddenly be lifted aloft to contemplate the entire course of the movement. All three are physically possible. Each seems to have been a planned situation of observation for the 1970 procession, because each observer saw a distinct processional shape.

I was not airborne at any point during the 1970 procession; hence, I must devise an airborne observer in retrospect—an easy task. An invented airborne observer looks down upon a map of Gloucester (Map 2) and sees the entire route of travel. This is the view which the city of Gloucester (or its responsible officials) had to take in order to clear the way for the procession's movement. The route was well known in advance and, seen from the air, it was significant. The procession was to move out of St. Peter's Square, up Washington Street, make a right hand turn on Middle Street to Dale Avenue and onto Prospect Street. The plan then called for the procession to travel Prospect Street downhill to where it meets Main Street, then continue down the full course of Main Street back to St. Peter's Square.

The route of the procession had several meanings. It encircled the whole of the old town of Gloucester, following old streets at some inconvenience. This was the Italian community's demonstration of its power in the city: it could claim the exclusive use of Gloucester's streets for several hours. The Catholic churches of Gloucester were connected by the procession's progress. The line of march was the shortest that could pass both St. Anne's Church and Our Lady of Good Voyage. The last leg of the route down Main Street passed through the entire region of Urban Renewal on its way to the Italian "West End" of Main Street and St. Peter's Club, finishing back at the square. The only message in taking the procession through the Urban Renewal zone was that nothing had changed: the buildings may have been taken down but the procession would continue to commemorate their sites. Or, perhaps it was plain conservative unwillingness to change the route. To a traffic-control officer, the pattern was a yearly headache. The intersection of Prospect and Main Streets was notorious for its congestion every Sunday throughout the summer. Normal Sunday tourist traffic exacerbated by fiesta-goers and an entire procession was "no merry-go-round," said the officer. "And it's a good day; that makes it worse." All the voices—Italian, Catholic, Gloucester—rose from the procession's route map.

A map is an ideal, and an airborne observer an abstraction. Even if the procession completed its route full around Gloucester, what fiesta is there in that? The plan is an anachronism, an intention to pour energy into maintaining a circuit that has always run that way.

On the ground, in 1970, the procession looked different. As the marching bands at the head of the procession started up and began to move, the secretary of St. Peter's Club glanced at them and pronounced, "That's no procession; that's a parade." And so it was. The procession had long since taken on the trappings of the American secular parade. It had acquired the parade's bulk, its secular noise, and its special problem of movement down urban streets. Gloucester's streets were too narrow to permit the passage of a parade, even without traffic. It was hard to exclude the traffic and impossible to divert it.

The first two bands took a roaring start out of St. Peter's Square only to stop abruptly before they had completed their first number. It was just traffic ahead that halted the march; it had taken some time to clear the altar, move the statue onto its carrying platform, secure it there, shoulder the platform and proceed into the procession. The bands moved up to a marching pace. Behind them came some local civic groups and Catholic religious organizations in full dress uniform, the Gloucester police force, the National Guard, the Boy Scouts, and the Knights of Columbus. Then a gap, an empty space in the parade movement, a simple void slowly reverting to pedestrian street traffic.

The people who were standing by the side of the street watching the passage of the bands began to move after the final contingent. They were enjoying the liberation of the street from traffic, taking a festive advantage of the space. If the forward part of the procession had been moving, they would have followed. The open space at the seeming end was static. People stood there holding it open for the space of a conversation. Children did what they are not allowed to do on city streets: they ran and chased each other randomly. Dogs appeared as they always do when there is an open space in the city.

Two men approached, one holding the Italian flag, the other the American. Directly after them came a float on the back of a truck. A

The float of the Pieta and Christ in glory.

child made up as Christ sat amid smaller children on a white-covered flat with a white curtain as a backdrop. Rows of artificial roses were strung along the sides and festooned across erect poles planted at each corner. "I suffer the little children to come unto me," read a banner above the tableau. The mothers of the children walked alongside. The second float was a tableau of the two remaining members of the Holy Family: Mary seated and mourning Jesus, Joseph standing and comforting her.

Another gap and then came a group of children carrying a banner, saying "St. Peter." From the distance, chanting could be heard. The parade effect abruptly ceased. The people on the road further down folded back onto the sides suddenly like water parting about the prow of a boat. The slow-moving mass of St. Peter shouldered by eight bearers made its progress up Washington Street toward the point where I stood. The crowd filling the open space drew itself out of the statue's path and formed a line along the side of the street. The approaching statue was the largest object in the procession; it gave the largest impression. The marching bands and the community powers that had preceded the statue composed people into a parade audience. St. Peter passed before the crowd—a juggernaut driving the people from its progress, even if they were already standing on the sides. Its force expanded in all directions and forced everyone behind and beneath it. Its size was overwhelming.

The statue was preceded by a pair of marshals who made sure that it moved ahead. Holding the front of the platform with two hands and walking backward was a committee member. He could not physically steady the platform but his necessarily slow walk gave the statue-carrying a uniform pace. His hands monitored the shifting balance of the weight as the groups went over the rough street bed of Gloucester. He shouted (in Italian), "Why are you all standing there with your mouths shut?" The repeated response "Viva San Pietro" intoned by all the men together synchronized their movement and gave relief from the burden. The tone and power of the chant described the statue's movement. Dressed in white, the men carrying the statue glowed in the brightness and heat of their effort.

The formerly passive crowd gained voice and action in the wake of the statue. Children holding long green ribbons attached to the statue walked behind the statue. Immediately following was a small corps of white-clad men and women who received contributions from the bystanders. A person in the crowd waved a bill to attract the attention of a collector, who took the bill and presented the giver with a St. Peter pin. The statue's front was already covered with bills contributed while the statue stood still on the fiesta altar and bills pinned onto ribbons trailed behind it.

Behind the statue followed marchers holding a flag, its center already weighted with coins tossed from the sidelines. Bystanders pitched coins and bills into the flag while siderunners deposited the contributions. A crowd of fishermen dressed in white were next in marching order. The bystanders turned in toward the marchers, calling to them. "Hey, Benny, how are ya?" "What, you in there too? I thought you laid off that saint stuff." "You get to carry the saint later?" "Hey, your wife says bring back something for the kids." Tension relaxed.

Next followed the Roma Band, slovenly holding instruments and slouching along the way. Familiar from many an Italian procession in Boston and environs, they received and acknowledged like celebrities the calls of people who did not know them. They contributed to the spirit of the procession in that they were a band appropriate to the familiarity that came in the statue's wake. They could be addressed as compatriots. "Look at that big guy, with the trumpet. He'd like to drink some *vino* at the club. Hey, you, come over to the club. Have a drink when you're done." The trumpeter acknowledged the invitation with a wave. The band took up their instruments and began to play "Santa Lucia" as though it were a new life coming into them.

Directly behind the Roma Band, following rather aggressively, were the Saugus Renegades, Vietnam veterans formed into a band. Dressed in flashy black and scarlet bolero outfits, they played a brassy rendition of the theme from the movie "The Good, the Bad and the Ugly." The bystanders were back to watching amd talking among themselves. They brought back the parade.

A group of white-clad teenagers followed carrying on poles a model seine-boat in which stood a statue of St. Peter. The statue was in green—an Italian color—and from his head fell two long green ribbons each held by a little girl in a white dress, walking on either side. The movement was accompanied by a squadron of dark-clad women guarding and keeping in order what clearly was their work. The audience cooed and made remarks appreciating the cuteness of the segment. It clearly was a community audience, one which recognized the meaning of this particular exhibit, but felt no obligation to participate in it beyond watching.

More tableaux vivants followed, floats borne along by trucks. The first, strewn with a superabundance of red roses, was "Mary as Queen of Heaven." A young lady sat modestly enthroned on a chair of gold and adored by three praying angels with silvery wings. The Virgin Mary is the guardian of the two main women's prayer organizations in the community. This was the work of one of them. The other organization, represented by the next float, could not compete by introducing another Virgin Mary but found the rather surprising subject of St. Joan of Arc. A child stood wearing foil armor and holding a *fleur-de-lis* banner, with a white-clad attendant standing on either side. On the float's backdrop was another large French crest. The float is not, however, a tribute to the city of Gloucester or to its French population. That St. Joan was inspired by a vision of the Virgin was insufficient to recommend her to the community's women.

At the point where Washington Street enters the center of Gloucester stands an equestrian monument of Joan of Arc. The monument marks the boundary of the extended Italian community, which presently occupies the slopes between Washington Street and Stacey Boulevard along the seafront. It was a private symbol of the Italian community grown away from the confines of the Fort and into the prosperity of the upper slopes. The imagery of conquest under the protection of the Virgin was then singularly appropriate to this demonstration. "The women like to dress little girls up as soldiers. There are a few every Halloween." An acquaintance in the crowd felt obliged to explain that the idea of a woman soldier appeals greatly to the community women. He was implying more than he said. The vision of the women who marched beside every float clarified the unspoken remainder: "Guardians."

The final float was in many ways a reversion. Eight boys dressed in yellow nor'easters sat inside a seine-boat gazing at a boy with a beard and green cloak, who stood in the prow holding the keys of St. Peter. Suspended from the mast above and attached fore and aft was a bright orange net filled with cardboard fish! The float of the Parisi family who own the marine supply store on Commercial Street, exhibited their main wares. Sporting the title "A Fisherman's

Dream," it was hard to tell whether the "dream" was the apparition of St. Peter to the fishermen or the entire exhibit of fishermen's accoutrements.

A symbol-hungry observer could easily make out a progress or regress in the mural of the parade. It started with the juggernaut of the statue, shrank to the smaller statue on the seine-boat and finally to the children's float of St. Peter. The saint became smaller, less imposing and more infantile. And he receded from statue to apparition. As the saint became less substantial, the motif of fishing grew until the full-sized boat on the final float dominated the scene. The saint receded into the past as fishing became of prime importance. It was a fantasy past, though, where seine-boats had masts and where nets were suspended like decorations in a tacky home bar. Children, who began the parade in precocious images of the Holy Family, ended it sailing off into dreamland. The whole cried for interpretation's unity.

Placing ethnography before personal comfort, I refused an invitation to go back to St. Peter's Club for a drink and vaguely hinted-at other emoluments. Prophecies of exhaustion and dehydration attended my refusal. ("You saw the thing. Nobody but the people in the parade go the whole route.") I caught up with the statue carrying group. It wasn't that I had suddenly become popular with the people; it was fiesta time and everyone was invited for a drink.

I had no trouble overtaking the statue-carriers. They were dragging up the slope to the level turn onto Middle Street. As they approached the turn, the group halted. The garage doors of the Madonna della Grazia Club had been thrown open, revealing the inner shrine of the Virgin all decked out in flowers and lights. While St. Peter paused, facing the opening for a few moments, one of the women guarding the shrine walked forward and placed an offering of flowers on the saint's platform. The male divinity was visiting the female. Silence reigned on both sides. Then St. Peter turned back to his procession.

As the statue made its way down Middle Street, few shouts greeted the fishermen or the collectors, and fewer contributions made their way onto the ribbons or into the banner. The people on the sides of the street were mere spectators, watching a parade. The parade marshals slowed the pace of the frontmost bands to close the gap between them and the statue. The whole line moved more tightly but also more slowly to the pace of the statue group. Shouts of "Viva San Pietro" were offered only sporadically. One of the white-clad carriers had been replaced by a man not in white—an unexpected change since the relief crew was waiting at the next stop and were all in white.

The floats, as they passed, received the greatest notice from the few people along the side of the street. By this time, not enough people stood along the sides of Middle or Dale Streets for the march even to amount to a parade, which requires a certain density and spirit of audience.

The procession's schedule called for a stop at St. Anne's Catholic Church on Prospect Street. The procession retreated up side streets to stand waiting while the statue was brought to the front of the church, where the monsignor recited a formula of blessing and sprayed holy water from an aspergil over statue and bearers. The traffic was released to move down the street during this ritual.

Italian saints' processions in Boston feature marching bands, corps of officials, and sometimes floats. But the saint's portion of these smaller processions is quite separable from the rest and constitutes a distinct processional unit that governs the rest. The primary role of the saint's party gives these processions their timing and form. While the bands wait, the saint is carried down narrow side streets to collect contributions given from doorways, or perhaps dropped from upper windows, to be pinned onto the ever-shaggier coat of bills. Their circuit completed, the carriers rejoin the bands to continue the main route of the procession-again-parade.

This does not happen in Gloucester. There are no narrow streets with tall tenements inhabited by Italian families in the area of Gloucester traversed by the procession. It has been a long while since the procession has taken the modest route of the Fort, where such tenement buildings have been abandoned or eliminated. Today, the splendor of the parade is suited to its imperial progress through parts of Gloucester not "controlled" by Italians. The only time the saint's party detaches itself is for the blessing at a church not considered an Italian domain. The Gloucester procession's determined straight line is a march of conquest, not a community procession. The display of power has superseded the display of community.

After the priest's blessing, the relief crew shouldered the statue

Children carrying a sheet into which coins are tossed.

and carried it back to the center of the road, which was cleared of traffic, thanks to the police. The other components of the parade emerged from their side streets and reformed the line of march. Some components had disappeared: the civic marching bodies were gone, as were most of the fishermen and the truckload of ballerinas at the end. Directly behind the statue walked a shoeless elderly man, holding a long candle lit against the steady sea breeze, and two elderly women, also with votary candles. They had all made vows (I learned by asking later) to follow the saint as far as they could. Statue-carriers had agreed to carry for them while they marched alongside. The small groups of onlookers watched this as they had watched the rest: with the indifferent, anonymous eyes of an audience to a spectacle, which concerns them as a spectacle alone.

The procession paraded down Prospect Street past the Portuguese church, Our Lady of Good Voyage. Here the procession met an explicit, sympathetic sort of spectatorship from the large crowd gathered before the church. A Portuguese flag was flying from the parish hall and the priest stood conspicuously among his parishioners. Here, the statue did not stop for a second blessing as had been the custom in previous years. Adequately forewarned, the police had kept the traffic at bay at the intersection of Prospect and Main Streets, and the procession moved on swiftly.

The plain gesture of sympathetic watching marked the outer limit of the procession as a progress past a point. From here it changed into the completion of a circuit. Those few spectators that remained followed the procession rather than stood watching it go by. The identity ever shifting between a passing spectacle and a moving thrust finally culminated into the thrust because there was no one to pass. As the procession reached the west-end section of Main Street, with its attenuated bunting, it had passed into the format if not the spirit of a cumulative procession. People who had begun watching the procession pass joined the line of march, while those who had been marching dropped off. The net effect was that by its end the procession became less and less formal. The children in the floats held their positions much more casually than they had at the start. The only section retaining its symmetry was the statue-carriers. They could hardly afford to do otherwise.

This moving crowd, with a semblance of bands and marchers around a statue, went past St. Peter's Club, into which a number of people disappeared.

Blessing and Mockery

Back in the square, the statue was deposited on a table at the foot of the altar stairs and stood facing out just above eye level. The chairs left from the Mass had been redistributed into small clusters like fossilized geometry of an earlier society. This society seemed to have lived in the altar space while the procession made its rounds and to have abandoned its arrangements after the return of the statue.

In the past, the procession made a circuit of the Fort, and the statue placed on Fort Beach facing seaward. In 1970 it stood in front of its altar looking landward over eddying sets of chairs and milling people eating lunches improvised from food stands. The carnival rides spun away. It was time for the blessing.

The blessing had two components. First, from a platform erected on the fringe of the carnival, overlooking Town Landing and all the boats docked there, Bishop Greco would deliver the Blessing of the Fleet. Then, from the altar a priest would conduct a benediction, which consists of a display of the Host within its golden monstrance.

The table in front of the altar still sold pins and programs and now chances in a raffle for a color TV set. Between the carnival and the altar space was an open area where people could walk and play freely. Embraces and running games were easier there than in the confined quarters of the carnival, where the constriction of space limited movement physically and socially. A fiesta-goer had to be serious about enjoyment to endure the carnival space for very long.

The loudspeaker announced that Bishop Greco would soon bless the fleet. All at once a crowd formed and began to move up Washington Street. There was considerable confusion about the location of Town Landing. Previous blessings had been conducted from a platform on Stacey Boulevard near the Fisherman's Statue. The fiesta program from 1969 said "just left of the altar at Town Landing," but it was not clear which left that meant. The fleet required a wide space, and Stacey Boulevard had a broad panorama of the harbor. I had a vision of the bishop casting his blessing over the ships assembled far over the open sea. So did many of the other people who started for Stacey Boulevard upon hearing that announcement. The fiesta had somehow encouraged that image in the minds of many people who were fully aware of Town Landing's location. The Fisherman's Statue also exercised its gravitational pull. This was the only event in the fiesta having to do with fishermen, and so it was a good idea to be near the statue and within clear sight of the sea.

Arriving there and seeing no platform and no bishop, we all paused for a moment. A man whom I had interviewed earlier said that the bishop would appear from a house across the way. I then remembered Town Landing and decided to trek back to St. Peter's Square. The spell ended for a few other people and we rushed back to St. Peter's Square, cameras in tow, joking over our foolishness in not knowing where the blessing was to be held. These people had attended the fiesta many times though they were not from Gloucester. "You never can tell when or where something's going to happen. They're always changing things around." In memory it becomes clear—that sole festive image of the bishop's operatic blessing, which never occurred but which I shared with others in acting as if it would. Carnival forms for a flash in this memory's merging of voices.

Back at the square, we found the bishop on a platform tucked into a corner of the carnival, surrounded on one side by a crowd densely packed and bristling with cameras and on the other by ships densely packed and bristling with masts. The photographic jumble labeled Blessing of the Fleet in fiesta literature was not just an epiphenomenon of poor photography. The blessing really looked squashed. The act itself was hardly distinguishable from the crowd observing it.

I know what happened, not because I saw it but because I knew that the same thing always happens. The bishop performed his blessing ritual and then descended into a boat to travel the harbor blessing boats as he passed them. The last sight to behold was the figure of the bishop disappearing beneath the platform. The roar of boat sirens announced that he was off. I imagined him cruising the waters of Gloucester Inner Harbor shaking his aspergil at fishing boats and yachts, but I did not see it.

Behind me in the altar space the Roma Band had finished its final selection and were packing up their instruments as the priest set up the instruments of the benediction on the altar table. The band's melodies had confirmed the ambience of ease in the altar space. People sat and ate their food or strolled around looking for others. The energetic knots of teenagers remained as they were after defecting from the morning Mass. When the choir, which had replaced the band on the altar, started to intone the introduction to the benediction, the teenagers actively mocked it. The deep-voiced singers who led the choir attracted their attention at first. They reproduced his tones and his facial contortions. Then they challenged the whole choir with a rival, rock rendition of the hymn. The priest continued the benediction mechanically, in spite of this commentary—or oblivious to it. Different voices speaking in the altar space did not add up to the fiesta. Though one was a parody of the other, neither had the other for an audience. There was no general audience. Only alternate performances.

I have no way of knowing if this tone of mockery has always arisen at the fiesta. No one remembers such things. Even those who mocked the solemn events in the past may simply equate such behavior with having a good time. My guess is that the mockery was probably always part of the festive sense. To assume that it was rebellion—the young against the old, the outsiders against the insiders—is fatuous. It sustained one group's participation in the fiesta without requiring explicit acceptance of any principle of festivity. It lead to an allover effect. It was not carnival. The benediction and the mockery of the benediction in the midst of an indifferent crowd was carnival.

Grease and Guts

The crowd was headed away from the square toward Pavillion Beach, where the sports events were scheduled to begin at five o'clock. The sound truck was already in place on the beach; the loudspeaker was launching its tirade against the boats in the harbor, asking them to clear out so the people onshore could view the greasy pole contest about to begin. The beach and the water were far more crowded than they had been on the rainy day before. The crowd on the beach (and certainly that in the boats) was certainly not just an expansion of the previous day's community crowd. It was composed of fiesta-goers. The Italian community, with its own oppositions, was a contingent within this wider mass, whose anonymity encircled and intensified the behavior of the Italians.

In between attempts to order the interfering boats out of the harbor, the speaker listed the contestants in the greasy pole contest. The list given in order contained many of the same names as the previous day, although there were more non-Italian names than

before: Cavanaugh, Benson, Grant, Sawyer. A few people in the
crowd repeated each of these names after the speaker with a question
mark at the end: "Cavanaugh? . . . His mother's Italian." "The
name was Italian but his father changed it. You know how it is."
This was true of two of the names, but other boys were high school
friends invited to take part in the contest, though not with the whole-
hearted approval of the fiesta committee. "What if one of them
wins? It's our contest." The same outlook that inspired the community elders' belief that St. Peter's High School was Italian rather
than Catholic (non-Italian Catholics had formed a sizeable portion
of the enrolment) caused them to believe that "Italian boys" were
still a distinct group. The composition of the greasy pole list was an
accurate reflection of a social reality which the voice of the
loudspeaker, "the community," disliked but allowed with paternal
indulgence.

The speaker also mentioned a few nicknames and added the status
of "former champ" or "1969 winner" to certain names. One
contestant, Mike Gellotti, was "walking for Sammy Balbo," a
former champ and now a partner in a local business. The principle of
substitution that applied to statue-carriers also operated in the greasy
pole contest. The speaker did not explain what was expected from
the substitution. Apparently everyone knew or did not care.

The contest began much to the speaker's expressed surprise just
shortly after five o'clock. Nickname, championship and sponsorship
accompanied each boy's name as he took his turn. The audience
gasped at each near miss, kept quiet for anything else. The speaker
provided a sports-like commentary. Again it remarked on any
inappropriateness: "What's an old married man like you doing out
there?" Again it singled out a walker who tried to sidle across the
pole rather than risk a run. "They tell me that's not the way to do it,
Steve. I don't know; I've never tried it." And the second time the
same contestant went (and failed) the same way: "They say you
don't make it like that, Steve. But you got guts just being out there."

"Guts" did seem to be the speaker's main issue. The boys were
out on the pole flaunting their courage. "Champ" status designated
a boy conspicuous for past display of guts. Someone who did not run
right across for the flag and the prize was deficient in guts, but (the
speaker conceded) he had never tried it himself, and besides, merely
taking the risk was a sign of guts. He recalled injuries sustained

during previous contests. Before the contest began the speaker had told the audience that the winner would receive the Salvatore Piscatella trophy. Piscatella had died serving his country in Vietnam. Guts clearly was the issue.

The list went through its first cycle with no success. Then through its second, also with none. Each time the speaker said the same things, for instance, promoting Gaetano Carini, the previous day's winner, as the one most likely to take the new title. As the cycle came around the second time, the speaker grew petulant, threatening to send the old champs from St. Peter's Club to finish the game off quickly. Boys were dropping out of the running or changing the order. The speaker enjoined them to stop until the order could be re-established. They stopped, then quickly resumed their disorder when given permission to start again. A quarrel broke out between the speaker and the boys on the pole. During a phase of abandoned running, one boy hit the pole hard and made the flag fall off. After a stunned pause, the speaker announced: "I'm told the greasy pole contest is over and that Salvi Benson is the winner because he knocked the flag down." The audience broke out into loud choral booing. After a hasty conference on the beach, the judges decided that the contest was not over; the loudspeaker retracted. "Would one of the boats out there please put the flag back on the pole? We like a nice, clean contest here." A boat put the flag back but the next boy knocked it off again. The audience cheered and the boat whistles blew with abandon.

The contest did have a highly attentive audience who could sway the judges and force the reopening of a decided contest. They followed the attempts with exhalations of breath. Even after the speaker became bored (and embarrassed at the poor performance), even after the boys themselves decided to have a free-for-all and knock the miserable flag down by any means, the audience kept a close eye on the procedure and would not agree to call the contest closed. The speaker and judges had to give in because, after all, they too were part of this audience, and a "nice, clean" game was an aspect of the ethos of "guts." The winner had to succeed by himself. The audience more than the contest managers themselves demanded a clear scene of courage before it could award a victory. One is reminded of Roman gladiator contests and the power of that audience. Of course, the greasy pole was much less lethal a game, completely unlike the war-in-miniature of the gladiators' arena.

The speaker announced that the winner of the greasy pole would receive the Salvatore Piscatella trophy at nine o'clock that evening in a ceremony at the altar.

Oarlocks

Preparations for the seine-boat race began immediately. This consisted of the speaker's reiteration of its exorcism to drive the boats out of the harbor and a listing of the crews of the three seine-boats. The speaker named the members of each crew, all Italian names with several nicknames among them. It drew notice to the one sixteen-year-old in a crew. In the Nina were the Gondolas, the runners-up in Saturday's contest; in the Pinta were the Young Scrod, the winners on Saturday; in the Santa Maria were the Vagabonds, the previous year's victors, racing for the first time this year. The captain of the winning team would receive the Frank D'Amico trophy, named after another Vietnam casualty.

The speaker announced that after the races there would be pie-eating and watermelon-eating contests and a one-legged race. A moment later it declared that these contests had been cancelled. It called upon the audience to purchase tickets for the raffle of a color TV set, on sale at the altar, and described the souvenir programs also available at the altar. It once again listed the seine-boat crews and the crews for the junior race.

It became clear that there was a problem. The three seine-boats were pulled up on shore and the crews gathered beside them, but there was no sign of the race beginning. The speaker admitted to the audience that the beginning of the race was delayed because some necessary equipment was missing: the oarlocks. "Does anybody in the audience have some oarlocks? We need oarlocks to row the boats. All we need is two oarlocks and we can get the race underway." The speaker remained silent for a time as if awaiting a univocal response from the audience. A man came walking to the loudspeaker stand calling: "If someone can get me the key I know where there are a lot of oarlocks, at least twelve of them there. Help me find my wife. She has the key." Another man lamented, "Nobody in the city of Gloucester sells oarlocks. We went to twelve different places. Nobody had them." The speaker repeated the request for oarlocks. The word "oarlocks" had through repetition (and weariness) begun to sag on the tongue. "Ollocks, does anybody have ollocks?'' The voice sounded strange and comical in its plea. Other voices in the audience were trying out the word.

The plot was laid plain. The oarlocks had been stolen in order to prevent the oarlock-less team from taking part in the race. "Whoever took the uhrlox please bring 'em back. We're in danger of having a two-boat race. They can't row without proper equipment.'' The Young Scrod were the team threatened with withdrawal. Conferences on the oarlocks went on beside the microphone. Runners came and went. A comic politics of oarlocks developed just on the fringe of the audience's awareness and in rhythm with the progressive distortion of the word.

If this were a novel, it would be possible to recreate the voices which sounded out during the oarlock quest. My notes tell me that a man quarreled with his wife, and a group of children claimed to know where the stolen oarlocks were hidden. The Young Scrod captain was publicly annoyed and accused the captain of the Gondolas of engineering the theft but the other captain remained nonchalant. But this is not a novel; it is structured memory tending toward ethnography. Hence, I may not invent voices I did not hear, especially if I induce these voices from the circumstances. I heard Scroddy Verga yell that each team should give up two oarlocks. I was not sure what that meant. Perhaps he wanted also to be in the carnival of using the word in public. As I write this, I repeat "oarlock" to myself aloud and I find that it does give a pleasure to the tongue for the first few times. The word itself is an archaeology of that festive moment. Officially, speaker and teams were annoyed by the problem and waiting for the race to begin; in actuality they were occupied with a treasure hunt for oarlocks all over Gloucester.

An oarlock is a stout metal pin surmounted by a metal crescent open at the top. The pin sits in a hole in the gunwale of the seine-boat, and the shaft of the oar rests in the crescent. The pin turns as the oar strokes, keeping the thrust of the oarsman from being expended in useless sliding along the side. Oarlocks are necessary for rowing with oars. Few people row with oars in the ocean today even for sport. Oarlocks are hard to find in seaport towns.

The above explanation, though not really necessary, is the best I can do to represent the obsessive need for the oarlock hunt. Eventually someone was successful and returned with the coveted equipment. Then the rowers swiftly positioned themselves and set out. The Young Scrod were ahead all the way and came in to shore at least three boat lengths ahead of the Gondolas. Amid the speaker's worried warnings to keep clear of the oncoming boats, the victorious Young Scrod wedged up onto the beach. "Scroddy" received the American flag followed by the Gondolas' Captain receiving the Italian flag. Part of the crowd began to funnel off the beach down Beach Court; a few people remained for the junior seine-boat races. The speaker declared that the pie-eating and watermelon-eating contests, as well as the one-legged race supposed to take place after the junior race, were cancelled. The fiesta had gone elsewhere.

Feast and Fiesta

The fiesta space exercised a strong draw as the day came to an end. The people returning from the beach and the smoothly finished junior seine-boat races came upon a party in progress that extended through the entire fiesta space between altar and carnival. Strewn across the altar space were cardboard boxes and wooden crates which were serving as chairs and tables for the people who had taken up a tenure in the space. Some of the tables were covered with meals improvised from the stands with the addition of food, dinnerware, glasses, and bottles imported from local kitchens. It was not a party but a feast, a set of little feasts culminating in the permissive atmosphere of the fiesta. Saint Peter, still in front of the altar, watched over this celebration.

Even then I recognized the *festa* from Pitre's descriptions. The open amiability, sharing of food, and most of all, the conduct of indoor activities outside were this festival. It was not a picnic, although many non-Italians could and did translate the celebration into a picnic of their own. They bought food and spread out napkins, crouching in an ungainly way to win atavistic contact with the earth beneath the asphalt. The Italians were not picnicking. Their makeshift tables replicated eating arrangements indoors. "Living outside" was an old theme of the fiesta. Before the statue ever appeared, this was the manner of celebration. If it were not for the rain, this scene probably would have been played Friday and Saturday nights as well, perhaps lasting all night.

The groups kept to their own separate settings, but they exchanged food with each other, and offered hospitality to bystanders. Out of the rigid linear time of the Mass and procession and sporting events had come this timeless gentle lasting feast. The voice of the community was loud with family and food. Yet the whole scene was quiet without giving the impression of a vaster celebration repressed. It was precisely timeless: no worry about this being the festive life of remote ages past. I think now, recalling this and trying to phrase it without ruining the flavor, that Rabelais and Bakhtin must both have known times like this, and in their rage to recover them, lost them in boisterous violence of imagery. Or perhaps this was the capitalist residue of that lost carnival. The rage, whether at the loss of carnival or of carnival bursting through, certainly did rise up, but not until much later. The utter consistency of this festive quiet wrapped the fiesta space.

The carnival rides next door were oddly in keeping with this generous mood. For the first time, as night fell, the carnival seemed part of the fiesta. Not only did people mount the rides, but they also experienced their sound, light and motion as part of the festive enjoyment. This was evident when, after dark on Sunday, the lights on the ferris wheel suddenly went out and the machine stopped. A deep gasp went through the entire fiesta space. It may have been fear for those on the ride, but it was too spontaneous to be actuated by reflection. It was a gasp of common acknowledgement that a piece had fallen from the fiesta. A man in the carnival cried, "Generator's out." After a few minutes the lights brought back the fiesta. How different a fiesta from the morning's Mass when the silence of the carnival was a condition of festivity! While that portion of the lights was dark, the fiesta ceased because attention focused upon that empty space. If the failure had lasted any longer than a few minutes, another festivity might have supervened.

Of course, there were small incidents and bits of speech that could be described. Their presence is anecdotal; it features the unity of celebration attained by the fiesta. Two bands positioned themselves on the altar and played alternately, quite consciously competing with each other for the greater volume and brassier display. Their music was simply the wallpaper of the inside, outside in the fiesta space.

The last formal events of the fiesta occurred on the altar, but in the midst of the people celebrating rather than before an audience. It was as if one of the groups there had become slightly more demonstrative than the others. A mild inflection of notice was directed toward the altar, but the fiesta was all family even for those who had none. The event that should have drawn the most excited audience, the drawing of lots for the color TV, simply occasioned a little polite applause when it was learned that the winner was Italian. The awarding of trophies followed. Each team member of the Young Scrod came to the microphone, identified himself, and made a little speech. The identification was intended to include everyone else momentarily in a conversation. As the men spoke, people in the crowd called out to them, asking personal questions. ("How's your daughter?" "What's happening up at the hall?"), which the speaker then answered conversationally. Each individual received hearty applause. In no way did this presentation alter the complexion of the gathering and its celebration. Gales of applause and shouted congratulations accompanied the bestowal of the D'Amico trophy. The men of the crew walked back into the crowd. The attempt to award the Piscatella trophy to the greasy pole winner was even more a function of the festive gathering. The man was not on the altar. He called out from one of the groups of teenagers on the side of the altar space that he would not come up to the altar to receive the award. The committee member handing out the trophies tried to persuade him, but he just shouted out his thanks and said he was glad that an Italian had won. The audience applauded his show warmly. The speaker then stated that the fireworks would begin soon on Pavillion Beach.

Groups walked to vantage points along Stacey Boulevard and the beach itself. The fireworks were in the air before people reached their stations. They were not very spectacular, nor were there many. They took place in another distant sky. There were some sparklers and Roman candles in anticipation of the Fourth of July.

Back in the fiesta space, the families were slowly dissipating. Over the loudspeaker came a call for men to help carry the statue back to its niche. The bands having parted, the scratchy recording of Santa Lucia came over the loudspeaker for the seemingly thousandth time. A group of men came from St. Peter's Club, determined to finish the work. Together with other recruits, they located the carrying poles, placed them through the platform and shouldered the statue. It rose unsteadily. As it did, two of the men began to chant "Viva San Pietro." The others, hesitantly and incredulously, took up the chant. The statue moved across the littered square followed by a small crowd of people also beginning to voice the chant. It sounded a cry in the emptying air, a cry which had all the sounds long dissipated but painfully rejoining at this final moment. It was a long, harsh, surrendering cry and in it were all the voices of the fiesta. This I recognized only later.

As the statue-carriers moved up Commercial Street buoyed by this cry, a group of teenagers on the sidewalk took up the sound and repeated it with an emphasis, mockingly sliding over the syllables "VIva San PiEtro, VIva San PiEtro." They grinned, joked, mimed the struggles of the carriers who were themselves weary and infirm with drink and other celebration. The mockery was not opposed to the chant of the carriers but extended it in one direction. Free of the burden of Saint Peter, they could shout this way. Yet in the teenagers' variation was the bitterness of feeling that weight might slowly descend upon their shoulders, too.

Saint Peter was carried back in honor, but he was also being cast off for another year. The pain of his dominance was going with the ponderous statue. The cry that accompanied the statue-carriers up Main Street to the front of St. Peter's Club was a cry at last of anguish at the departure of Saint Peter and the fiesta he had brought. But it was not that simple. The statue disappeared into the door of St. Peter's Club and then reappeared in its window shrine. The crowd held for one gigantic minute, then melted into people walking away.

PART FOUR

EPILOGUE

CHAPTER 10

Closure

Since conclusion is a recognition of closure achieved, there are many ways to conclude the 1970 St. Peter's Fiesta. Each register of voices had its closure and thus conclusion, all united in the common end of ending the fiesta. It even seemed that the voice of closure had, like the author's voice in a modern novel, become one voice among the many, reciting its intent in the fiesta itself. The rain always threatened to end the fiesta and leave it incomplete; Sunday's clearing finished the fiesta by completing its weather and confirming the adage that the sun always shines for Saint Peter. The issue of weather was enough. The sporting events formed a progress and an assurance of closure, from the eliminations on Thursday to the award of the trophies on Sunday evening. The sporting events were the fiesta closing upon itself.

Reflections

However complex and multiply meaningful a participant's sense of the fiesta during its performance, no single theme or event made the fiesta a whole. Indeed, the fiesta argued against consummation throughout its entire course but then succumbed to it all the way through. At the fiesta opening, the dignitaries, politicians and clergy were making a closure as they stood on the bandstand and acknowledged that the fiesta could have a beginning and it was their responsibility, as officials, to provide that. Yet several of the figures mentioned were not on the bandstand, and some standing there did their best to subvert their distinctiveness by siding with the audience. Closing the fiesta required separating a formal schedule of events (sports, procession) from an anonymous mass of ongoing happenings (carnival, feasting); it required distinguishing a set of named fiesta performers (officials, contestants) from an audience. Those charged with executing the closure constantly placed it at risk while they were at the task. The loudspeaker alternated irregularly between being a performer, a paternalistic voice of authority, and a projection of the audience. The greasy pole performers themselves took on the attributes of an audience. All the care with names—the membership in some mysterious inner circle projected by the listing of nicknames—was for nought when the boys began to run on their own. Once someone finally did dislodge the flag it was impossible to tell who had accomplished the feat. When the trophy was awarded at the fiesta closing, the winner was not on the bandstand but in the audience, from which his voice was heard. The stage for closure was a stage for resisting closure. The resistance had to give way, however, to the inevitable ending. The winner in the audience on Sunday evening had already left the fiesta while those on the stage carried it on.

Closure spoke and was heard. The line of events was drawn firmly across the four days of the fiesta. There were periods of faintness when the fiesta retired inside and left the outside events in suspension, times when it was apparent to the audience that there was much more to the fiesta than the printed schedule. But if possible, the fiesta followed its line from one display to the next. The times given on the schedule were seldom accurate. The loudspeaker's remark when the Sunday sports actually did begin "on time" reveals that, however haphazardly events took place, the organizing powers always had the schedule before them. They always envisioned a bounded agenda. Family feasts and private parties, weddings and worship services all went on alongside the fiesta, but they were dependent on the ideal of the fiesta as a series of single events, which had changed but slightly since 1929. Whatever closure each individual found in the fiesta, it depended on the achievement of the fiesta schedule. People might retire to intimate family spaces, but they had always been able to do that; the fiesta was plein air and public, striving to win that condition against weather and privatism as it had when first performed.

The possibility that the 1970 fiesta might close all fiestas, might be the last, was part of its consummation. The letter from a committee member, written to the *Gloucester Daily Times*, saying that the possible demise of the fiesta, was "no joke" was brought to mind again on the Monday night following the fiesta when a drunk lobbed a brick through St. Peter's glass window and damaged the statue. No one, drunk or not, had ever assaulted the statue before, and though the man had no more than drunken motives, the vulnerability of the fiesta was clearly linked with the statue's vulnerability. Sam Favazza, the statue's owner and chief inspiration of the fiesta, was in his nineties and unable to attend the fiesta in 1970, because he was recuperating from major surgery. The expenses of the fiesta were increasing with inflation. Already some events that had been added during the 1950s, the pie-eating and watermelon-eating contests and some childrens' races, had ceased. The number of people who had seen the fiesta's beginnings was diminishing yearly; those who had known it all their lives complained that it was degenerating. The transition from yearly closure to historic closure was a clear possiblity, and the prospect of ultimate closure filled participants' experience of the 1970 festival. The chorus of boys mocking the re-enshrinement of the statue on Sunday night was the voice of this final closure.

That mocking chorus can be seen as closure in a number of different ways: as a profane inversion of fiesta sacredness within the precincts of the fiesta's providing an internal closure in line with the clowns' performance on Saturday; as a release of energy finally turning destructive in the drunkard's brick on Monday night; as a text of youthful male resentments against the adult male establishment symbolized by Saint Peter. Mocking a sacred figure fits into pious Catholic imagery of Calvary and martyrdom; inverting an elevated figure belongs to the imagery of revolution. Depending upon where one stood, any of these closures might have presented itself and seemed absolute. They are not just different meanings of the same event, or different readings of the same text—textuality is just alternative—but orders of fiesta experience. They are voices calling for closure and, one of them, for a final closure.

The survey of voices of the 1970 fiesta, which is the focus of this book, bespeaks many conclusions, any of which can be taken as The Conclusion. The participant's experience and requirements decide that. As much as anyone else at the fiesta, the anthropologist is determined to reach a conclusion. The only difference may be that she/he must conclude within the mainsteam of anthropological theory in order to satisfy colleagues. The anthropologist has the dialectic, a pleasing intellectual turn, to command and her/his own voices to hear. But hearing these voices concludes the fiesta for the anthropologist as for anyone else.

Hearing the 1970 fiesta as a text of the Italian community's current state is one possibility. It is tempting to read the fiesta as a failure reflecting the community's failure. The ever-weakening fisheries, the urban renewal of the downtown, and the treacherous sale of St. Peter's High School were all individual signs of social disorganization, for which the fiesta in its disrupted action provided a text. The community's problems were not symbolized outright in the fiesta action; they were not acted out. Together, they contributed to the failure to accomplish the unification and celebration of community, which the fiesta promises yearly. The fiesta is predicated upon a community which did not exist in 1970: the 1970 fiesta took place but failed. The disorganization of the sporting events, the disintegration of the Mass and the frequent exhibits of irreverence were symbols of this failure. Reading the 1970 fiesta as text leads to this conclusion.

But the fiesta was a failure only to someone who needed that kind of closure, perhaps in response to outside events, perhaps because of being a connoisseur of chaos. The fiesta might fail this way every year; it might have been failing continuously from the start. The atmosphere of failure, with its threat of termination, is cathartic in a way that happy success cannot be. The flaw in the failure reading is a flaw of reading in general: it presupposes the classical reader's omniscience and dawning idea of the interconnectedness of all things. Closure is in the reading itself. Thus we conclude that the fiesta has failed because it looks that way, because people tell us so, because there are suggestions in the order of society that all is not right. Reading texts is a closed system that leaves aside much experience.

The idea of reading culture as text(s) implies its own completeness and, having been accomplished, its own necessity. Conclusions derive from a logical exhaustiveness that quickly pervade the entire event. The fiesta may have been a failure for some participants, perhaps even in the way described above, but such an interpretation is ultimately only one voice heard in the fiesta. Those who heard it assumed sufficiency and necessity; it was their experience of the fiesta to assume that.

This argument sounds like the equivocations of theoretical pluralism: any conclusion is acceptable and is as good as any other. This is not a tenable conclusion. I have already hinted broadly that voices of catharsis, release, inversion are heard in this fiesta too, at times very strongly, but none of these voices seems to urge itself upon the hearer like that of textuality. It is as text that the fiesta makes itself most audible. The underhanded functionalism of that voice is part not only of theory, but also, in 1970, of the fiesta experience.

Echoes

The 1970 fiesta performance can be read in relation to other texts, other performances of the same fiesta. The "failure" reading juxtaposes the 1970 performance against an ideal successful performance which never took place. Many other real performances did take place. I described a succession of fiestas leading up to 1970, thus introducing a history of fiestas and the obligations of historical narrative into this study. Fifteen years have come and gone since 1970 and, yes, fifteen fiestas. The historical narrative I have inadvertently begun has to be completed: the 1970 fiesta potentially makes sense as a text leading to later texts. One wants to know what has happened to the Fiesta since 1970, because writing it down has made it a romance to be concluded by further reading.

During the winter of 1970-71 the offshore platform where the greasy pole contest takes place came down in a gale. No one undertook to restore the platform until the verge of the fiesta, and then it looked as if the committee could not meet the expenses of the restoration, estimated at $3,000. For the first time, the cost of the fiesta was made public among calls for stepped-up contributions. (In the past, the statue had been covered with five and ten dollar bills but lately, complained Committee Chairman Gaspar Lafata, "It's been more like one dollar bills.") The marine contractor called to repair the platform agreed to do most of the work as a contribution to the fiesta, but as the time approached he had not completed the work. Lafata was determined to hold the greasy pole contest: "We leave this out this year and next year something else will be left out. The next thing you know they won't have a fiesta" (personal communication, 1971). A complex arrangement was worked out: the contractor temporarily sold the fiesta committee his barge for one hundred dollars. The contest could then take place without his having to buy expensive insurance.

A car narrowly missed people in a fiesta crowd. During the procession the Saugus Renegades, living up to their name, broke away from the line of march and gave an impromptu performance of Jesus Christ Superstar. Archbishop Medeiros, Cardinal Cushing's successor, delivered the Blessing of the Fleet but after he embarked into the harbor to bless the individual boats the plywood platform erected for the blessing collapsed under the weight of the crowd. No one was hurt. Salvi Benson won the greasy pole contest. The reunited Young Scrod came in first in the seine-boat races. The Vietnam war continued.

In 1972, money was again the most serious problem. The committee estimated their total outlay at $20,000. The Matarazzo brothers, who followed the family tradition of setting up the lights and the outdoor altar, nearly withdrew from the fiesta. The cost of the lighting had risen from $200 to over $5,000. They could not manage on the sum the committee allowed them. A woman walked in the greasy pole contest on Sunday but Salvi Benson won once more. The barge with the fireworks sank.

The 1973 fiesta was riot-torn. A scuffle outside a Main Street bar early Saturday morning turned into a confrontation between police and a rock-throwing mob. Rain on Saturday quieted things down, but trouble started up again when the weather cleared at night. The committee closed the fiesta early that Saturday, and the return of the statue to St. Peter's Club on Sunday "seemed to break the tension." Police arrested a total of 75 persons, blaming the lower drinking age (reduced from 21 to 18 in an effort to keep teenagers from driving out of state for alcohol) and the management of Fats Walla's bar. "If you blame fiesta for what happened last week," said Mr. Lafata, "what are you going to blame when it happens again next week?" Later that year, Sam Favazza died.

The 1974 fiesta was decreed the Fiesta of Peace at the conclusion of peace in Vietnam and at the expectation that the previous year's events would not be repeated. Police on duty throughout the weekend had no trouble. Salvi Benson won the greasy pole contest yet again, and the All-Beefers won the seine-boat race. The procession was the longest ever, and the audience, estimated at fifteen thousand, the largest ever. The carnival rides were inspected. Only three fishing boats were present for the blessing; the rest were pleasure boats. The smaller number of fishing boats in the fleet meant less income for the fiesta.

An ABC camera crew filmed a staged greasy pole contest on Wednesday prior to the fiesta in 1975. Salvi Benson "lost" the real contest on Sunday, at last. The pleasure boats were in every way a nuisance, crowding the harbor and displacing the buoys marking out the seine-boat course. A number of the old hands in the statue-carrying squad had retired, passing the honor down to their sons. Again, there was discussion of ending the fiesta, so great were the costs.

In 1980, Johnny Parisi, who had been chosen captain of the statue-carriers after Sam Favazza's death, was still serving in that capacity. He said he had a long waiting list of people who wanted to carry the statue on Sunday. He described his technique of walking along with the statue, whistling "one to get ready, two to go," to keep time with the chant. No one had ever fallen or stumbled carrying the statue. Joe Frontiero, a long-time greasy-pole veteran, recalled the past, when the award for walking the pole had been $20, which he rapidly drank away at St. Peter's Club. They played a game "guinea up, guinea down" in which the contestant tried to drink an entire bucket of beer without taking a breath. There had never been a serious injury on the greasy pole, he maintained; everyone wore clothes to cushion the impact of the fall. No one walked for the money, he declared; they walked for Saint Peter.

Heavy boat traffic in the harbor dominated the 1984 Fiesta. A crowd of nearly two thousand attended the outdoor Mass. Portuguese-American fishermen carried Our Lady of Good Voyage statue in the Sunday procession. There was a large field for the Fiesta Five, the five-mile race down Stacey Boulevard in which olympic finalists and college athletes competed. During the awards ceremonies on Sunday evening, prizes were awarded for the greasy pole contest, the seine-boat and (motorized) lobster-boat races, and for the footrace. The refreshments were provided by McDonald's.

The 1985 fiesta was strikingly similar to the one I had observed 15 years earlier. It began with heavy rain which resolved itself into a splendid sunny day for the procession. I obtained photographs, which revealed impressive continuities in the fiesta tradition. I came to realize that the cry "Viva San Pietro" was more than a desire to perpetuate the saint's memory and paternal protection. It was also a wish—sometimes vociferous, sometimes muffled—that a celebration could somehow transcend and transfigure the changes that had shaken its social foundation.

Themes sounded in the 1970 Fiesta repeated themselves and grew louder over a constant sound. The fragility of the fiesta equipment and of the fiesta itself were symbolized in the collapsed greasy pole platform, the collapsed platform used for the blessing, and the sunken fireworks barge. The one rock thrown through the saint's plate glass window turned into droves during the riot. The nearness of fiesta bankruptcy showed in one aspect, then another. But peace finally came. The Vietnam war, always a submerged voice in the 1970 fiesta, roared out and was silenced. The passing of the old guard, Sam Favazza, and the death or retirement around the same time of several statue-carriers coincided with the violence of 1973. The growing inconvenience of the crowds, on land and then at sea, a rumor in the 1970 fiesta, has become the main trouble of the fiesta. The events are diluted by the masses of people who appear just to watch them. At the same time, the events themselves are decreasingly Italian: Portuguese appear in the procession, a Mexican piñata has been introduced, and there is a new footrace in which a special prize has to be set aside for the Italians.

There are continuities that have become historical: the greasy pole, which seems more central across time than it did in one performance, and the statue, vulnerable but with the strange power to quell riots by its departure. And Bishop Greco, who will continue to deliver his sermon as long as he may.

The text of the fiesta holds together as the intrustion of the mass expands it to the breaking point. All the voices of the fiesta are fainter now as the anonymous mass of vast motley variegation arrives larger and larger each year. And the fiesta is closed not by one event or gesture, not in the acceptance of any one concluding voice, not in the end of the fiesta performances, but by being consumed.

References

Abrahams, Roger
  1972   "Christmas and Carnival on St. Vincent." *Western Folklore* 31:275-289.
Alpers, Svetlana
  1983   "Interpretation without Representation or, the viewing of Las Meninas." *Representations* 1:31-42.
Babson, John J.
  1860   History of the Town of Gloucester, Cape Ann. Gloucester: Procter Brothers.
Bakhtin, Mikhail
  1968   Rabelais and His World. Helen Iswolsky, trans. Cambridge: MIT Press.
  1973   Problems of Dostoyevsky's Poetics. R. W. Postel, trans. New York: Ardis.
Barber, C. L.
  1959   Shakespeare's Festive Comedy: A Study of Dramatic Form and Its Relation to Social Custom. Princeton: Princeton University Press.
Bartlett, Kim
  1977   The Finest Kind: the Fishermen of Gloucester. New York: Norton.
Bauman, Richard and Roger Abrahams
  1978   "Ranges of Festival Behavior" IN Barbara Babcock, ed. The Reversible World: Symbolic Inversion in Art and Society. Ithaca, New York: Cornell University Press, pp. 171-84.
Belo, Jane
  1966   Bali: Temple Festival (Monographs of the American Ethnological Society, 22). Seattle: University of Washington Press.
Bharucha, Rustom
  1984   "A Collision of Cultures: Some Western Interpretations of the Indian Theatre." *Asia Theatre Journal* 1:1-20.
Bodde, Dirk
  1975   Festivals in Classical China. Princeton: Princeton University Press.

Boon, James
  1982   Other Tribes, Other Scribes. Cambridge: Cambridge
          University Press.
Brown, Norman O.
  1959   Life Against Death. New York: Vintage.
Burke, Kenneth
  1945   A Grammar of Motives. Berkeley: University of
          California Press.
Butcher, S. H.
  1951   Aristotle's Theory of Poetry and Fine Art. New York:
          Dover.
Caillois, Roger
  1961   Man, Play and Games. Glencoe, IL: Free Press.
Canetti, Elias
  1984   Crowds and Power. Carol Stewart, trans. New York:
          Farrer, Straus and Giroux.
Cantor, Milton and Bruce Laurie, eds.
  1977   Class, Sex and the Woman Worker. Westport, CT:
          Greenwood Press.
Chapman, Charlotte
  1971   Milocca: A Sicilian Village. Cambridge: Cambridge
          University Press.
Cohen, Abner
  1980   "Drama and Politics in the Development of a London
          Carnival." *Man* (ns) 15:65-87.
  1982   "A Polyethnic London Carnival as a Contested Cultural
          Performance." *Racial and Ethnic Studies* 5:23-41.
Cohen, Miriam
  1977   "Italian-American Women in New York City, 1900-1950:
          Work and School." IN Milton Cantor and Bruce Laurie,
          eds. Class, Sex and the Woman Worker. Westport CT:
          Greenwood Press, pp. 120-43.
Connolly, James B.
  1904   The Seiners. New York: C. Scriber's Sons.
  1927   The Book of the Gloucester Fishermen. New York: John
          Day.
  1930   Gloucestermen. New York: C. Scriber's Sons.
Crapanzano, Vincent
  1973   The Hamadsha. Berkeley: University of California Press.

Davis, Natalie
1984 "Charivari, Honor, and Community in Seventeenth-Century Lyon and Geneva." IN John MacAloon, ed., Rite, Drama, Festival, Spectacle: Rehearsals Toward a Theory of Cultural Performance. Philadelphia: ISHI, pp. 42–58.
De Conde, Alexander
1971 Half Bitter, Half Sweet. New York: Scribner's.
Dewar, Margaret
1983 Industry in Trouble: The Federal Government and the New England Fisheries. Philadelphia: Temple University Press.
Diggin, John
1972 Mussolini and Fascism: The View from America. Princeton: Princeton University Press.
Erikson, Eric
1950 Childhood and Society. New York: Norton.
Frazer, James George
1919 The Golden Bough, Part V: The Scapegoat. London: Macmillan.
Freud, Sigmund
1920 Beyond the Pleasure Principle. James Strachey, trans. New York: Liveright.
Furst, Peter
1972 Flesh of the Gods: The Ritual Uses of Hallucinogens. New York: Praeger.
Gambino, Richard
1974 Blood of My Blood: The Dilemma of the Italian-Americans. Garden City, NY: Doubleday.
Geertz, Clifford
1972 "Deep Play: Notes on the Balinese Cockfight." *Daedalus* 101:1–38.
1980 "Blurred Genres: The Refiguration of Social Thought." *American Scholar* 29:165–179.
Gilbert, Katherine Everett and Helmut Kuhn
1972 A History of Aesthetics. New York: Dover.
Gluckman, Max
1963 Order and Rebellion in Tribal Africa. Glencoe, IL: Free Press.
1965 Politics, Law and Ritual in Tribal Society. New York: Mentor.

Hawes, C. B.
1923   Gloucester By Land and By Sea. Published by the author.
Hawthorne, Hildegarde
1916   Old Seaport Towns of New England. New York: Dodd, Mead.
Hyman, Stanley E.
1962   The Tangled Bank: Darwin, Marx, Frazer and Freud as Imaginative Writers. New York: Atheneum.
Jensen, Albert C.
1972   The Cod. New York: Crowell.
Ladurie, Emmanuel Le Roy
1979   Carnival in Romans. Mary Feeney, trans. New York: George Braziller, Inc.
Lavenda, Robert
1983   "Family and Corporation: Two Styles of Celebration in Cental Minnesota." IN Frank E. Manning, ed., The Celebration of Society: Perspectives on Contemporary Cultural Performance. Bowling Green, Ohio: Bowling Green University Press and London, Ontario: Centre for Social and Humanistic Studies, pp 51–64.
Leach, Edmund
1961   Rethinking Anthropology. London: Athlone.
Lincoln, Bruce
1985   "Revolutionary Exhumations in Spain, July 1936." *Comparative Studies in Society and History 27:241-60.*
MacAloon, John
1981   This Great Symbol: Pierre de Coubertin and the Origins of the Modern Olympic Games. Chicago: University of Chicago Press.
Malinowski, Bronislaw
1922   Argonauts of the Western Pacific. New York: Dutton (1961).
Manning Frank E., ed.
1983   The Celebration of Society: Perspectives on Contemporary Cultural Performance. Bowling Green, Ohio: Bowling Green University Press, and London, Ontario: Centre for Social and Humanistic Studies.
Marriott, McKim
1966   Village India: Studies in the Little Community. Chicago: University of Chicago Press.

Meltzer, Michael
  1980   The World of the Small Commercial Fishermen: Their Lives and their Boats. New York: Dover.
Moore, Sally F. and Myerhoff, Barbara G.
  1977   Secular Ritual. Amsterdam: Van Gorcum.
Nash, June
  1979   We Eat the Mines and the Mines Eat Us: Dependency and Exploitation in the Bolivian Tin Mines. New York: Columbia University Press.
Nelli, Humbert S.
  1964   "The Italian Padrone System." *Labor History* 5:153–67.
Nietzsche, Friedrich
  1967   The Birth of Tragedy and The Case of Wagner. Walter Kaufman, trans. New York: Vintage.
Ostor, Akos
  1980   The Play of the Gods: Locality, Ideology, Structure, and Time in the Festivals of a Bengali Town. Chicago: University of Chicago Press.
Peacock, James
  1968   Rites of Modernization: Symbolic and Social Aspects of Indonesian Proletarian Drama. Chicago: University of Chicago Press.
Pétonnet, Colette
  1982   "L'observation flottante. L'exemple d'un cimetière parisien." *L'Homme* XXII, 4:37–47.
Piaget, Jean
  1951   Play, Dreams and Imitation in Childhood. C. Gattengo and F. M. Hodgson, trans. London: Atherton.
Pitre, Giuseppe
  1881   Spectacoli e feste popolari Siciliani. Torino-Palermo: Carlo Clausen.
  1900   Feste patronali in Sicilia. Palermo: Luigi Redone.
Pringle, James
  1892   History of the City and Town of Gloucester, Cape Ann, Massachusetts. Published by the author.
  1923   Gloucester: A Pageant-Drama of New England's Oldest Fishing Town . . . Gloucester: Published by the author.

Procter, James G.
  1873   Fisherman's Memorial and Record Book. Published by the author.
  1874   Fishermen's Ballads and Songs of the Sea. Compiled by Procter Bros., Gloucester, Massachusetts: Procter Bros.
  1882   The Fisherman's Own Book. Gloucester, Massachusetts: Procter Bros.
Rappaport, Roy
  1968   Pigs for the Ancestors. New Haven: Yale University Press.
Sartorio, Enrico
  1918   Social and Religious Life of Italians in America. Boston: Christopher.
Schechner, Richard
  1977   Essays on Performance Theory. New York: Drama Books.
  1981   "The Ramlila of Ramnagar." *The Drama Review* 21:251-82.
  1982   "Ramlila of Ramnagar and America's Oberammergau." IN Victor Turner, ed., Celebration: Studies in Festivity and Ritual. Washington, D.C.: Smithsonian Institution Press, pp. 89-106.
Schieffelin, Edward
  1976   The Sorrow of the Lonely and the Burning of the Dancers. New York: St. Martin's Press.
Sutton-Smith, Brian
  1980   "A Sportive Theory of Play." IN Helen Schwartzmann, ed. Play and Culture. West Point, NY: Leisure Press, pp 10-19.
Tedlock, Dennis
  1983   The Spoken Word and the Work of Interpretation. Philadelphia: University of Pennsylvania Press.
Turner, Victor
  1969   The Ritual Process. Chicago: Aldine.
  1974   Dramas, Fields and Metaphors: Symbolic Action in Human Society. Ithaca, New York: Cornell University Press.
  1977   "Variations on a Theme of Liminality." IN Sally Falk Moore and Barbara Myerhoff, eds. Secular Ritual. Amsterdam: Van Gorcum, pp 36-51.
  1978   (and Edith Turner) Image and Pilgrimage in Christian Culture. New York: Columbia University Press.

1981   The Drums of Affliction. Ithaca, New York: Cornell University Press.

1982   (ed.) Celebration: Studies in Festivity and Ritual. Washington, D.C.: Smithsonian Institution Press.

1983   "Carnival in Rio: Dionysian Drama in an Industrializing Society." IN Frank E. Manning, ed. The Celebration of Society: Perspectives on Contemporary Cultural Performance. Bowling Green, Ohio: Bowling Green University Press, and London, Ontario: Centre for Social and Humanistic Studies, pp. 103–124.

Walens, Stanley

1981   Feasting with Cannibals: A Study in Kwakiutl Cosmology. Princeton, NJ: Princeton University Press.

Warner, William Lloyd

1959   The Living and the Dead: A Study of the Symbolic Life of Americans (Yankee City Series, Vol. V) New Haven, CT: Yale University Press.

Webber, J. S.

1885   In and Around Cape Ann: Handbook of Gloucester, Massachusetts and Vicinity. -ublished by the author.

Yans-McLaughlin, Virginia

1977   "Italian Women and Work: Experience and Perception." IN Milton Cantor and Bruce Laurie, eds. Class, Sex and the Woman Worker. Westport, CT: Greenwood Press, pp. 101–19.

Author Index

Subject Index